DESIGNERS: Ezequiel Galasso,
Galasso Guitars (Argentina)
DISTRIBUTOR: Galasso Guitars
YEAR OF DEVELOPMENT: 2011
MAIN MATERIALS: recycled skateboards
MAIN GREEN STRATEGIES: recycled material, local production,
durable

**Design:
Ezequiel Galasso,
Gianfranco De
Gennaro Gilmour**

PHOTOS: IGNACIO MORREST

Karton Design

The lightness and natural appearance of cardboard offers unlimited application opportunities. These objects are formed by folding cardboard and are constructed of tightly fitted boards. This individual, handmade cardboard furniture range, including lamps, chairs, tables and vases, offers an interesting furniture solution for apartments, offices or shops. The unusual material choice reflects the designer's belief that people are open to new solutions and ideas, willing to embrace stunning yet functional designs.

DESIGNERS: János Terbe/Karton Design (Hungary)
DISTRIBUTOR: János Terbe
YEAR OF DEVELOPMENT: 2000
MAIN MATERIALS: carboard, textile
MAIN GREEN STRATEGIES: recycled materials, local production

**Design:
János Terbe**

Brut

Brut is a monolithic set of stool and barbecue for outdoor use, produced by casting a compound of cement and coconut coir, an agricultural waste. This material is water and fireproof. The designer explores the field of self-production by creating a low-tech casting process, using accessible products, most of them available at Ikea stores. The mix is compressed into a reusable mold, which is actually a domestic plastic container. This fibrous compound is so strong that doesn't need any inner reinforcement. A Styrofoam core reduces the weight of each piece significantly, making it possible to be lifted by a single person. The unique texture of the pieces defies the cold roughness of concrete, as the result of using recycled coconut coir as the main ingredient. The process allows the possibility of producing these durable pieces on a small scale, locally and at an extremely low cost.

DESIGNERS: Agustina Bottoni (Italy/Argentina)
YEAR OF DEVELOPMENT: 2012
MAIN MATERIALS: portland cement, coconut coir, styrofoam, steel
MAIN GREEN STRATEGIES: recycled material, use of agricultural waste, local production, self-production, durable, low energy consumption

**Design:
Agustina Bottoni**

Glitch Collection

Ryan Frank is a South African designer who specializes in designing sustainable furniture. Whilst developing the Glitch Collection, he followed his holistic intentions to create timeless furniture that can be completely upcycled or rather reused over and over. Ryan Frank used reclaimed steel frames and bamboo surfaces to construct this furniture range and developed a technique that does not use any glue or screws, so that the pieces can be dismantled again easily. Talking about his work, the designer makes point of utilizing only salvaged materials.

DESIGNERS: Ryan Frank (United Kingdom)
DISTRIBUTOR: Ryan Frank
CLIENT: Glitch Lab
YEAR OF DEVELOPMENT: 2012
MAIN MATERIALS: bamboo, cork, steel
MAIN GREEN STRATEGIES: renewable, recyclable, durable, biodegradble

Design:
Ryan Frank

PHOTOS: RUBEN ORTIZ. PORTRAIT: PAOLOVEGLIANI

Terra Stools

Terra is a brand that produces bio furniture and artifacts from compressed earth and agricultural waste. Terra Stools are part of a series of organic products and furniture made from earth and natural fibers. This range is 100 percent organic and requires zero energy, does not cause pollution and is fully renewable and compostable. Terra's objects are produced using a compressing process that combines indigenous knowledge and contemporary production methods. At the end of their lifecycle, the products can either be remodeled by the user or simply composted and used in the garden. Terra's vision is to set the standard for local production and local use, using only locally available material and organic waste.

Design: Adital Ela

DESIGNERS: Adital Ela/S-Sense Design (Israel)
YEAR OF DEVELOPMENT: 2012
MAIN MATERIALS: earth from construction waste, straw,
agricultural waste materials
MAIN GREEN STRATEGIES: compostable, zero energy production,
recyclable, local production

PHOTOS: SHAY BEN EFRAYIM, PORTRAIT: DAPHNA KAPLAN

Cesaria Evora

This storage unit was conceived as a way
to reuse empty steel cans. The unit is
composed of several cans, glued together
to form different shapes or clusters that
can hold socks, underwear, fruit, keys,
etc. The piece was always intended as
a DIY project, where the end-user makes
a storage unit with their own discarded
cans. A PDF with instructions has been
available from the designer's website
since 2004.

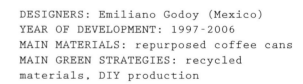

DESIGNERS: Emiliano Godoy (Mexico)
YEAR OF DEVELOPMENT: 1997-2006
MAIN MATERIALS: repurposed coffee cans
MAIN GREEN STRATEGIES: recycled
materials, DIY production

**Design:
Emiliano Godoy**

PHOTOS: DANTE BUSQUETS. PORTRAIT: ENRIQUE MACÍAS

Funky Chair

Funky Chair is a modular seating system, different from conventional furniture. The system's lightweight units and separate cushions create a very flexible seating arrangement, which can be adapted to suit living spaces of all sizes. The design is intended specifically for cramped living conditions. The user can simply add more units if circumstances change and more space becomes available. New cushions can be added as armrests or can be used freely on the floor.

DESIGNERS: Onur Y. Demiroz/OYD design (Turkey)
YEAR OF DEVELOPMENT: 2009
MAIN MATERIALS: plywood, aluminum, double-layered foam, fabric
MAIN GREEN STRATEGIES: separate cushions, modular, recyclable

FL Inout Chair

FL Inout Chair is a comfortable lounge chair that is easy to use and aesthetically pleasing. The FL out-chair comprises a web of polyester and a frame made of wood-plastic composite material. The FL in-chair is formed by an additional cushion tied with straps underneath the web. By using wood-plastic composites (WPCs), the side frames are molded and the tubes are extruded without any post-processes after molding. The flat-pack chair can be easily assembled at home and requires only eight screws. It weighs 6.5 kilograms and can be used outside or inside, as WPCs are weather resistant.

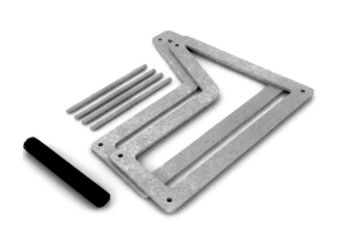

DESIGNERS: Onur Y. Demiroz (Turkey)
YEAR OF DEVELOPMENT: 2012
MAIN MATERIALS: wood, plastic
MAIN GREEN STRATEGIES: recycled materials

Pulpop MP3 Speaker

Environmentally and design conscious, this USB MP3 speaker is made of recycled pulp. It has an unusual donut shape and is ultra light, despite its appearance. The vibration inside the hollow space amplifies the sound. After a series of trial and error processes, this speaker is surprisingly effective and produces good quality sound.

DESIGNERS: Balance Wu (USA)
DISTRIBUTOR: MollaSpace
YEAR OF DEVELOPMENT: 2012
MAIN MATERIALS: recycled paper pulp
MAIN GREEN STRATEGIES: recycled materials

**Design:
Balance Wu**

Repurpose

Repurpose Inc., is a leading innovator of premium, eco-friendly food service products for consumers. Repurpose was founded with a mission to eliminate single use plastics and replace them with renewable plant based alternatives. The company's goal is to bring every consumer a high-quality, compostable, sustainable option and help them lower their carbon footprint at an affordable price.

DESIGNERS: Repurpose (USA)
DISTRIBUTOR: Repurpose Compostables
YEAR OF DEVELOPMENT: 2009
MAIN MATERIALS: plants (corn)
MAIN GREEN STRATEGIES: recycable,
renewable, compostable, BPA-free

FS Chair

The idea behind the FS chair is to minimize the use of resources but maximize function. The chair is made of birch plywood panels and very little material is wasted. It can be shipped as flat-pack, reducing shipping costs, energy and pollution. The chair is easy to assemble and does not use any screws or glue. The design is inspired by the shape of a ribcage, evenly supporting the load. A storage space is also provided underneath the seat, housing a pouf for a versatile and innovative seating experience.

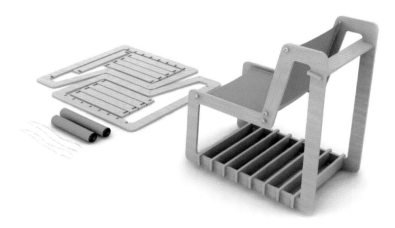

DESIGNERS: Onur Y. Demiroz/OYD design (Turkey)
DISTRIBUTOR: OYD Design
YEAR OF DEVELOPMENT: 2011
MAIN MATERIALS: Plywood, organic fabric, rope
MAIN GREEN STRATEGIES: low energy consumption, biodegradable

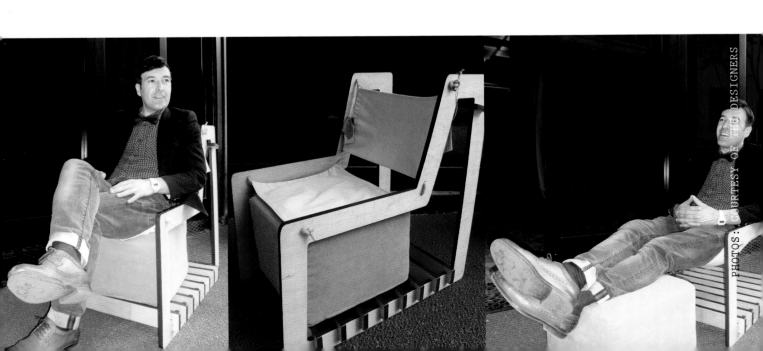

PHOTOS: COURTESY OF THE DESIGNERS

Cabinet Knobs

Design: Leilani Norman

SpectraDécor was established in 2002 by Seattle artist Leilani Norman to create design-focused decorative hardware, based on her experience with metals and clay. By 2004, Leilani changed the direction of the studio toward USA-made, eco-friendly materials and processes. Two of the studio's environmentally-friendly knob and pull collections, Castaway and Beach Pebble, feature USA-made metal bases and 100 percent recycled glass. The two collections were inspired by the simple beauty of found glass. Castaway's translucent, matte colors are reminiscent of beach glass, softened by wave action over time. Beach Pebble mimics the opaque colors of pebbles found at rivers and beaches. SpectraDécor hardware is meticulously hand-crafted. Every knob, pull and handle is created with care by skilled hands. Artisan quality and dramatic visual impact describe the studio's eco-friendly products.

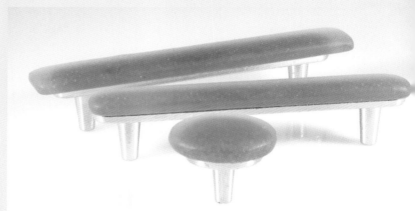

DESIGNERS: Leilani Norman (USA)
DISTRIBUTOR: SpectraDécor
YEAR OF DEVELOPMENT: 2012
MAIN MATERIALS: recycled glass
MAIN GREEN STRATEGIES: recycled materials,
locally sourced materials

PHOTOS: RODRIGO DEMEDEIROS, PORTRAIT: NIZAR MARAR

Autarchy

Autarchy pays homage to the uncomplicated, the simple and the everyday.
The product range includes a collection of functional and durable vessels and lamps. Naturally desiccated
or baked at low temperatures, each item
is made with a bio-material composed
of 70 percent flour, 20 percent agricultural waste, and 10 percent natural
limestone. The differences in the col-
or palette are obtained by the selection of distinct vegetables, spices and
roots, which are dried, boiled or fil-
tered for their natural dyes. The product range is an open source where information and knowledge are shared. The
name Autarchy suggests an alternative
way of producing goods, where inherited
knowledge is used to find sustainable
and uncomplicated solutions.

DESIGNERS: Studio Formafantasma (The Netherlands)
DISTRIBUTOR: Studio Formafantasma
YEAR OF DEVELOPMENT: 2010
MAIN MATERIALS: flour, agricultural waste, limestone, colour obtained
by filtering and boiling vegetables and spices
MAIN GREEN STRATEGIES: local, low energy consumption

PHOTOS: STUDIO FORMAFANTASMA. PORTRAIT: DELNO LEGANANI SISTO

Produktwerft Series

The Produktwerft Series enhances used and antique materials with new clear-cut design. Working in close collaboration with a recycling company, furniture and accessories are saved and revived. Each product resulting from this upcycling process is environmentally friendly, and sustainable. The material tells its own story. The aim is not to hide the scratches and signs of use, but to make them the focus of the design.

DESIGNERS: Sascha Akkermann/Studio Sascha Akkermann (Germany)
DISTRIBUTOR: Produktwerft
YEAR OF DEVELOPMENT: 2013
MAIN MATERIALS: reclaimed wood
MAIN GREEN STRATEGIES: recycled wood, 100% handmade

**Design:
Sascha Akkermann**

Otarky Rocking Chair

This project was part of the designer's final project at university. This human-powered rocking chair can generate energy through the rocking motion. Aesthetically, the chair design is a modern reinterpretation of the classic rocking chair. The combination of metal and wood with elegant flowing lines give the chair a minimalistic elegant appearance. The generator itself is hidden in the chair rockers.

**Design:
Igor Gitelstain**

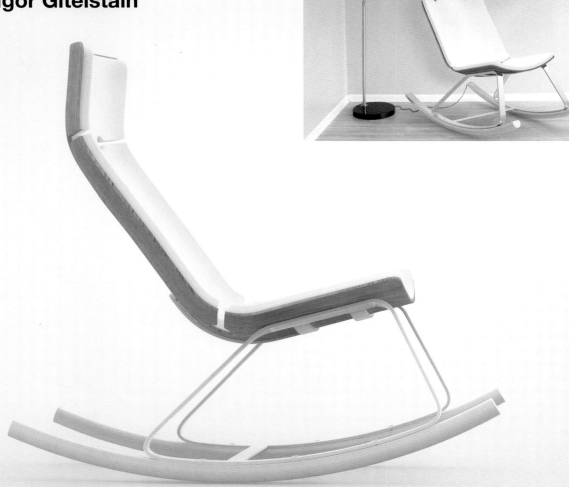

Linear electricity generator

Coil inductor
Magnet
Ball bearing

DESIGNERS: Igor Gitelstain (Israel)
YEAR OF DEVELOPMENT: 2012
MAIN MATERIALS: laminated wood, steel,
magnet, copper
MAIN GREEN STRATEGIES: energy generation

A Switch

"A switch to sustainable rattan production and supply" is a WWF project co-funded by the European commission. The overarching aim of this project is to improve the rattan production system at all levels, from harvesting done by local communities, pre-processing, processing and production. The project discourages export of raw material and encourages rattan processing to achieve more profitable refined products.

Inspiration for the designs was found in traditional carpentry handicraft found in both Europe and South Asia. The rattan furniture was constructed with dowel joint techniques to exclude additional material such as nails and screws. The technique minimizes the use of material and creates the simple design.

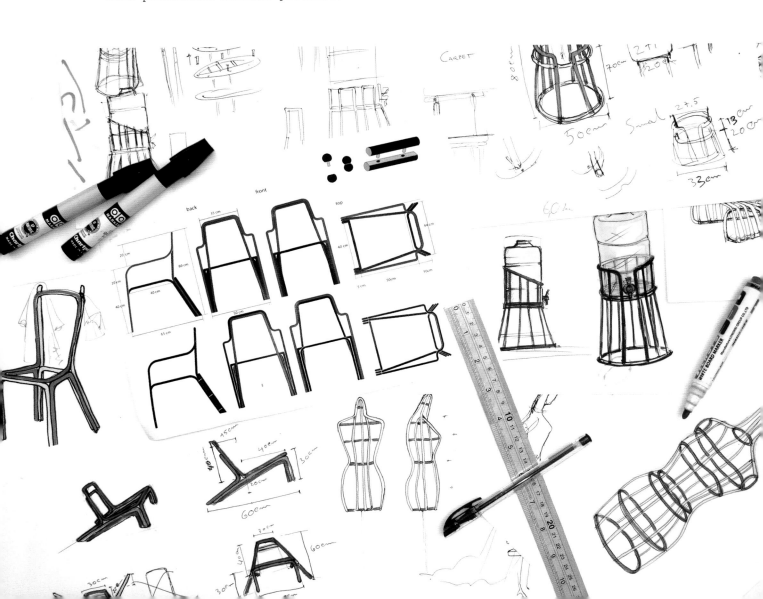

Design: Per Brolund, Em Riem

DESIGNERS: Per Brolund, Em Riem (Sweden/Cambodia)
DISTRIBUTOR: Rattan Association of Cambodia (RAC)
YEAR OF DEVELOPMENT: 2011
MAIN MATERIALS: rattan
MAIN GREEN STRATEGIES: local production, low energy consumption, capacity
building, product life cycle and logistics, cleaner production

Roadsign Art

This is a self initiated project that transforms old roadsigns and timbers into contemporary artwork. The artist came across large amounts of disused signs in council depots which were destined to be scrapped. Previously a graphic designer, the artist applies a graphic sensibility to the arrangements which also highlight the intricate surface textures that have built up on the materials over time.

DESIGNERS: Brett Coelho (Australia)
DISTRIBUTOR: Brett Coelho Studio
YEAR OF DEVELOPMENT: 2012
MAIN MATERIALS: recycled road signs
MAIN GREEN STRATEGIES: recycled materials

Design:
Brett Coelho

Living Pots

Design: Hakan Gürsu

Designed to reduce tree consumption in plant growing and cultivation, Living Pots are sustainable cultivation units that are comprised of 100 percent recyclable and reused materials. Made out of simple bent metal pieces and wood scraps, the product is flat-packed and can be easily assembled. Especially convenient for mushroom cultivation on logs, the units can also be stacked to save space. A standard unit is one meter in length, however units can be cut to the required length and packed. Turning scrap logs into a sustainable and decorative product, this unit is a minimalist end product for environmentally conscious growers who wish to reduce their carbon footprint.

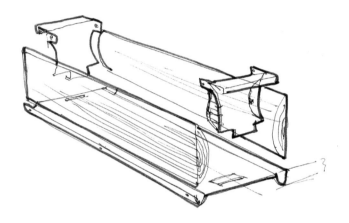

DESIGNERS: Hakan Gürsu/Designnobis (Turkey)
YEAR OF DEVELOPMENT: 2012
MAIN MATERIALS: scrap wood, sheet metal
MAIN GREEN STRATEGIES: 100% recyclable, low energy consumption, recycled material

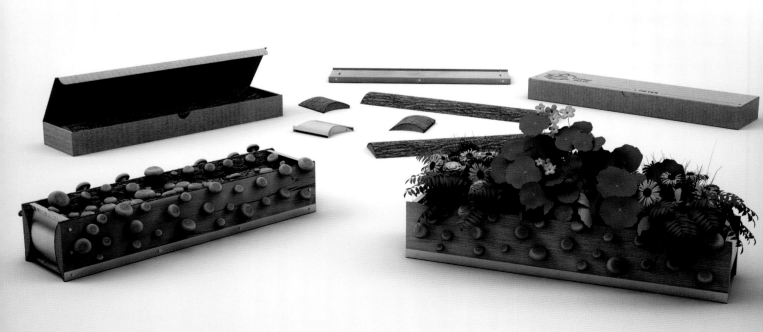

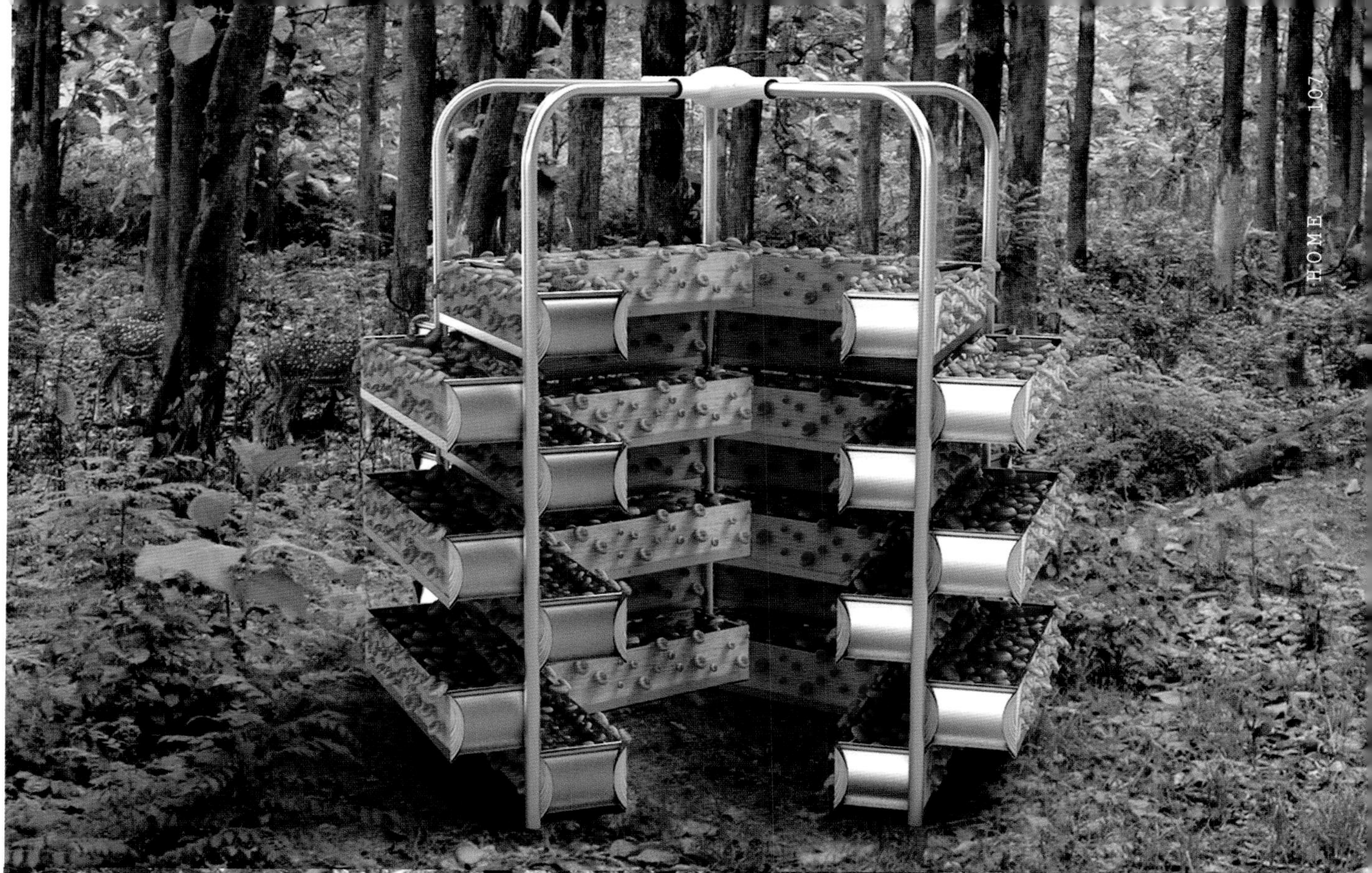

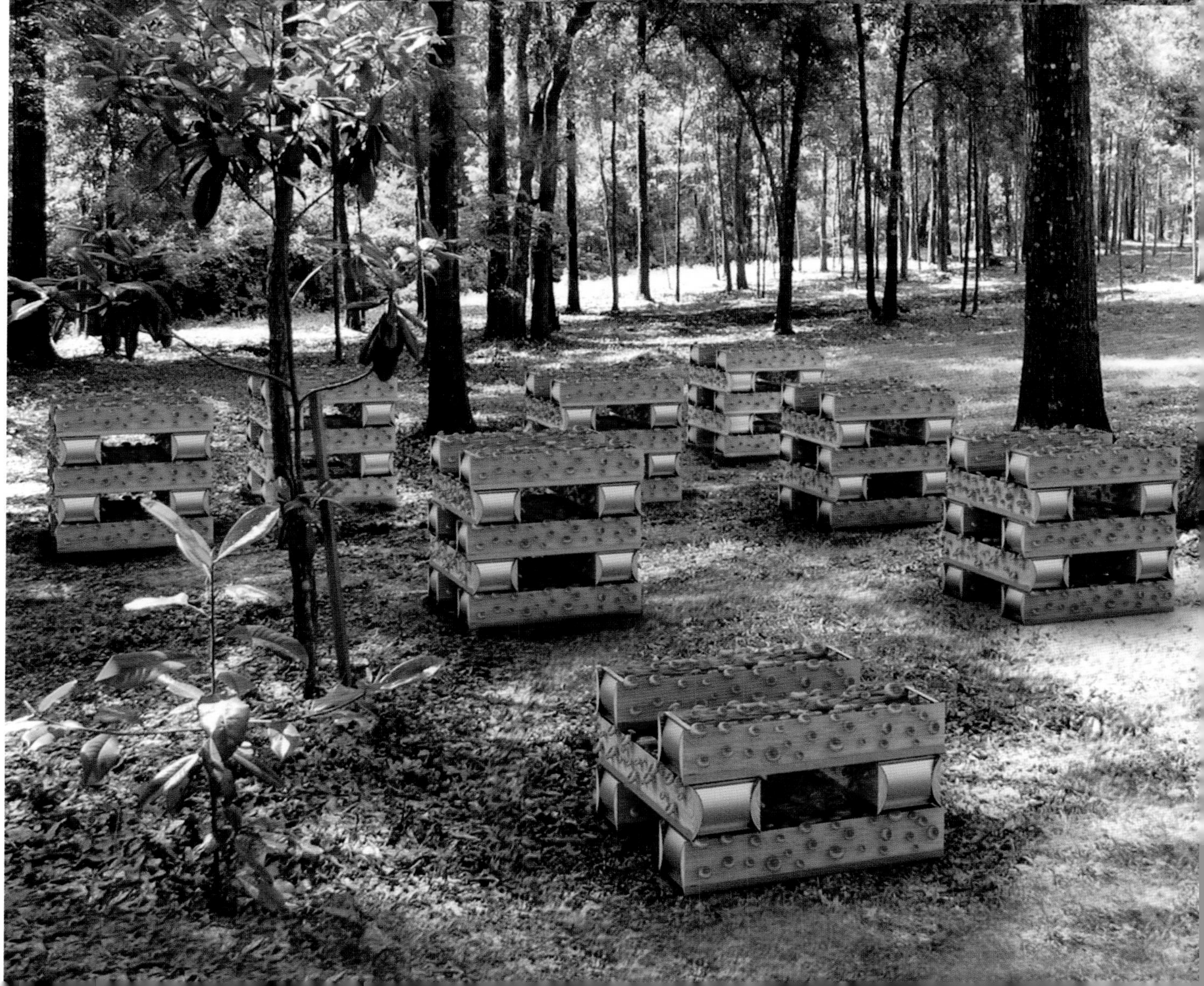

PHOTOS: COURTESY OF THE DESIGNERS

Auxano

Design: Philip Houiellebecq

Auxano was designed to enable the ever-increasing amount of city dwellers to grow their own produce effectively and efficiently within the space constraints of city living. Auxano is an innovative and practical solution, which revolutionizes the current indoor hydroponics market, providing very economical vegetable and herb growth rates through maximizing exposure to sunlight. This has been achieved through mounting growing units on windows. Its innovative oxygenating pump system further enhances its green credentials in that no electricity is needed to operate the product.

DESIGNERS: Philip Houiellebecq
(United Kingdom)
YEAR OF DEVELOPMENT: 2012
MAIN MATERIALS: recyclable plastic, wood
MAIN GREEN STRATEGIES: recyclable materials, local production, enhances self-sufficiency

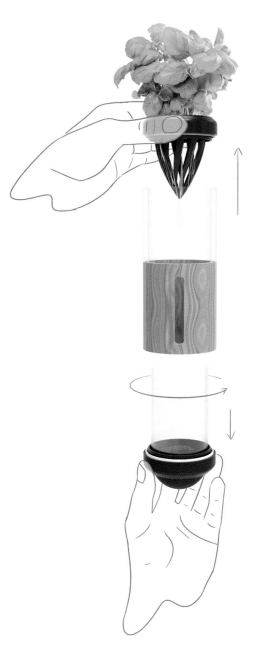

Design: Mani Mani

Owl

Owl is a smart pendant light with light sensors, energy efficient LED bulbs and a multi-platform smart phone app. Owl the smart light, comes with an app for iPhone, Android and Blackberry devices as well as a web interface for any web enabled device through a web browser. The interface allows the user to adjust the color temperature; warm to cool white, and the intensity of the light with a dimmer effect directly from their handheld device. This smart environmentally conscious system will provide the user with the energy consumption reading in real time. With different profiles and settings the user can create a new profile or select a pre-set program to adjust the systems behavior according to their daily use.

DESIGNERS: Mani Mani/Fishtnk Design Factory (Canada)
DISTRIBUTOR: Fishtnk Design Factory
YEAR OF DEVELOPMENT: 2012
MAIN MATERIALS: LED lighting, wood, plywood frame with aluminum detail
MAIN GREEN STRATEGIES: low energy, green energy monitoring system, reusable components, local manufacturing, FSC certified materials

Waste Less Log Chair

This chair is made of a single oak log. The design was inspired by waste wood, left over from timber log processing. The designers came up with a way to make use of this wasted timber, creating a garden chair that integrates two seating options; either as a rocking chair or with a foot rest. The design retains the inherent simplicity of the material, using only rudimentary joins and fixtures. The outer segments of the raw oak log are joined together with simple iron treads. Each position can be fixed manually, by moving the iron clamps, which are themselves inspired by the tools used in timber industry to move logs. When not in use, the chair can be completely closed. As the chair is for outside use, the closed position solves the problem of winter storage.

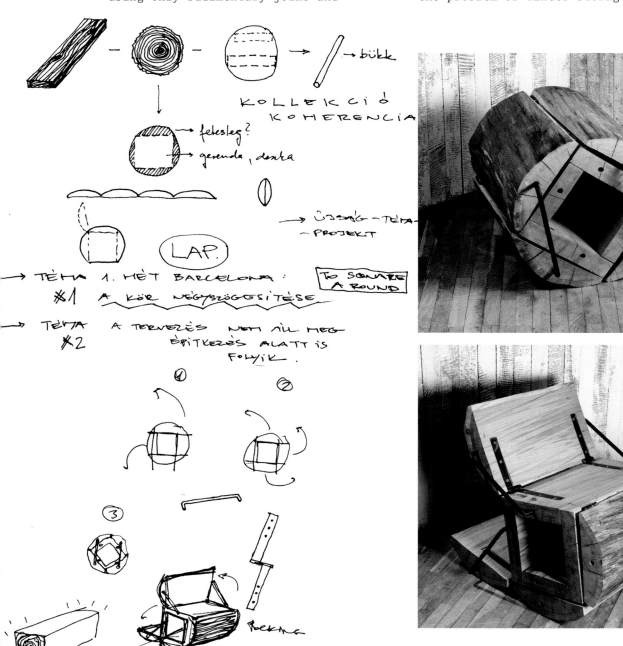

Design: architecture uncomfortable workshop

```
DESIGNERS: architecture
uncomfortable workshop (Hungary)
DISTRIBUTOR: architecture
uncomfortable workshop
YEAR OF DEVELOPMENT: 2012
MAIN MATERIALS: wood, iron
MAIN GREEN STRATEGIES: local
production, low energy, natural
materials, 100% recyclable
```

PHOTOS: DÁNIEL DUTKAI

Wanda

Design: Nicoletta Savioni, Giovanni Rivolta

Wanda is a chaise longue made of recycled cardboard cutout-shapes, with felt fitted to the seat top. The sides are finished with MDF-lacquered panels. The shape of the chair is designed to fit the curves of the body, supporting the weight comfortably and evenly. The white colors combined with brown tones give the chairs an elegant and natural appearance and a muted character that can blend in with almost any living environment.

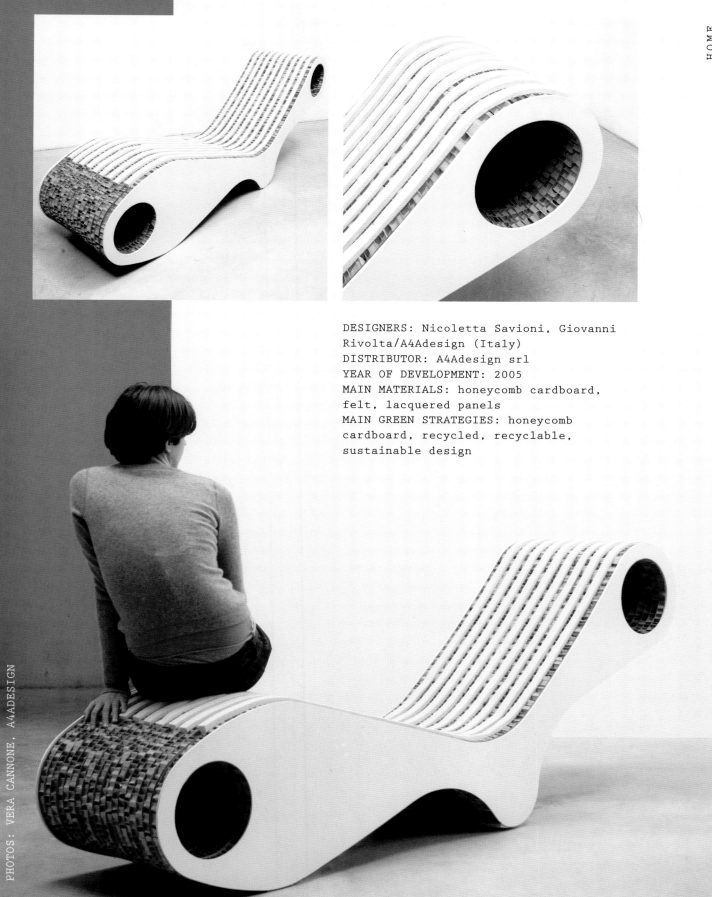

DESIGNERS: Nicoletta Savioni, Giovanni
Rivolta/A4Adesign (Italy)
DISTRIBUTOR: A4Adesign srl
YEAR OF DEVELOPMENT: 2005
MAIN MATERIALS: honeycomb cardboard,
felt, lacquered panels
MAIN GREEN STRATEGIES: honeycomb
cardboard, recycled, recyclable,
sustainable design

Pet-Tree

Design: Hakan Gürsu

Pet-Tree is a vertical planting system made from re-used PET containers and recycled plastic pieces. Using waste plastic bottles as pots, the design enables growing a wide range of plants in a small space. The system uses its tree-like form for water circulation and harvests rainwater while feeding plants through drip irrigation. Reducing energy consumption in terms of material usage, water and effort, Pet-Tree uses waste plastics to support nature. The flat-pack set serves as an option for organic growers in urban spaces or can be used in industrial agriculture as modular greenhouses. The design has been honored in Urban Sustainable Design and Rural Sustainable Design in International Design Awards and Green Dot Awards.

DESIGNERS: Hakan Gürsu/Designnobis (Turkey)
YEAR OF DEVELOPMENT: 2010
MAIN MATERIALS: recycled PET bottles, recycled plastics, stainless steel tubes
MAIN GREEN STRATEGIES: reuse of PETs, recycled materials, low energy consumption

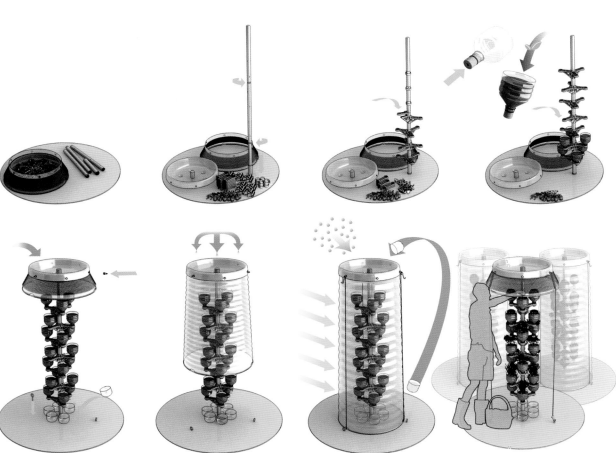

Earth Block

Earth Block is a collection of blocks made from biomasses that can be stacked together to create various structures. The blocks are made from natural materials, such as coffee beans, tree bark or natural sawdust. The raw materials are collected from a variety of regions and environments, making each block a unique piece with its own distinctive look. The recycled raw materials are dried and fractured, then mixed with a binding material (polypropylene) to create the blocks. The Earth Block collection comes in two different sizes. The small ones are available in natural sawdust, natural coffee bean and tree bark. The larger blocks comprise plain wood, brown or black tree barks.

Design:
Masaya Akiyama

DESIGNERS: Masaya Akiyama/Colors (Japan)
DISTRIBUTOR: Colors
YEAR OF DEVELOPMENT: 2011
MAIN MATERIALS: natural sawdust, natural
coffee bean skin, tree bark
MAIN GREEN STRATEGIES: biomass, recycled
materials, local production

PHOTOS: SHOICHIRO NAKAMURA

WineHive Modular Wine Racks

The WineHive was designed by John Paulick, an award-winning industrial designer, based in Philadelphia. Paulick's patent-pending interlocking joint design allows WineHive to be comprised of just a single structural element that repeats itself to form an infinite array of honeycomb structures. The key design principle behind the honeycomb structure is the 120-degree joint system, which disperses weight loads far more efficiently than man-made 90-degree structures, while using much less material. It also creates perfectly modular hexagonal shapes that nest beautifully with one another. Combine that with flat-pack shipping and durable, locally produced recyclable aluminum, and you've got yourself a very 'green' wine rack.

DESIGNERS: John Paulick Design (USA)
DISTRIBUTOR: WineHive
YEAR OF DEVELOPMENT: 2012
MAIN MATERIALS: extruded recyclable aluminum
MAIN GREEN STRATEGIES: recyclable, flat-pack shipping, local production, durable

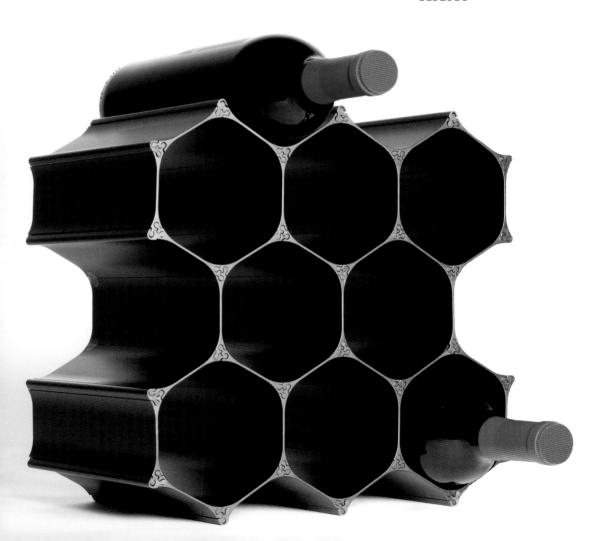

**Design:
John Paulick**

PHOTOS: MARK HAVENS. PORTRAIT: SARAH FERENZ

Ménage à Trois

In Ménage à Trois, the designers convert an non-recyclable object, an old refrigerator, into a funky sofa. The design takes advantage of the original shape of the refrigerator to minimize waste. The finishing is done with eco friendly resin and VOC-free black paint. A reading lamp was also added in the space that held the original fridge lamp.

The lamp is created from an leftover industrial string roll and a flexible metal tube. The fridge is mounted on a metal structure with wheels to ensure stability and mobility. Finally, the cushions are made from a discarded PVC advertisement banner and the filling from an old sofa.

Design: Transfodesign

DESIGNERS: Transfodesign (Spain)
DISTRIBUTOR: Transfodesign
YEAR OF DEVELOPMENT: 2011
MAIN MATERIALS: discarded refrigerator,
discarded PVC advertisement banner,
cushioning foam, LED light, discarded
industrial string roll, flexible metal
tube, wheels
MAIN GREEN STRATEGIES: reuse of non-
recyclable waste, recyclable, local
production, durable, sustainable

Barrel Tables

Each piece in this range of furniture was once a strong Swiss wine barrel. The barrels were no longer useable for wine storage but the designer recognized that the wood could still be put to good use. With a lot of care and attention, new life has been breathed into the old wood, resulting in stunning and unique pieces of furniture, full of history and character.

Design: Walter Amrhyn

PHOTOS: Walter Amrhyn. PORTRAIT: STUDIO ONE

DESIGNERS: Walter Amrhyn (Switzerland)
DISTRIBUTOR: Walter's Wood Idea
YEAR OF DEVELOPMENT: 2007
MAIN MATERIALS: oak wood from wine barrels
MAIN GREEN STRATEGIES: recycled materials,
local production

Havearest

The Havearest series of furnishings comprises an armchair and two-seater sofa made from recycled and recyclable cardboard that are assembled by simply dovetailing the pieces together with water-glue. Havearest is aimed at the retail, events and contract sectors because it comes into its own in large spaces that make the most of its geometric silhouette and scenographic potential. It was tested in Milan during the September 2012 Fashion Week, when it was given a sneak preview at the inauguration of the Patrizia Pepe showroom in the prestigious former Palazzo delle Poste, an historic Post Office building.

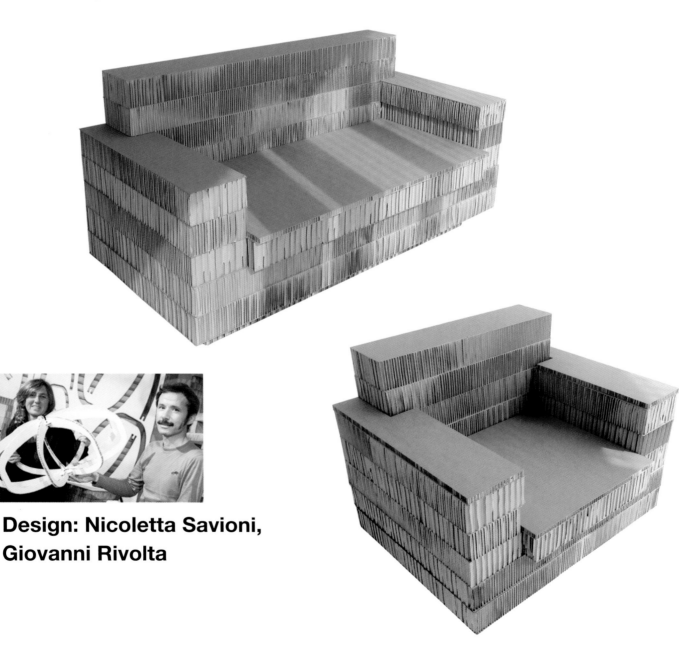

**Design: Nicoletta Savioni,
Giovanni Rivolta**

DESIGNERS: Nicoletta Savioni, Giovanni
Rivolta, Markùs Stefànsson/A4Adesign (Italy)
DISTRIBUTOR: A4Adesign srl
YEAR OF DEVELOPMENT: 2012
MAIN MATERIALS: recycled honeycomb cardboard
MAIN GREEN STRATEGIES: recycled, recyclable,
sustainable design

Canyon Collection

Inspired by the sculptures and infinite layers of the American Grand Canyon, this eco-friendly collection designed by architect Giancarlo Zema for the new Origami Furniture brand consists of a chair, coffee table and lamp made of recycled cardboard. Soft and curvaceous shapes reveal cosy niches to store bags, magazines or small objects. Designed to furnish the trendiest indoor areas in an environmentally friendly and innovative way.

Design:
Giancarlo Zema

DESIGNERS: Giancarlo Zema Design Group (Italy)
CLIENT: Origami Furniture
YEAR OF DEVELOPMENT: 2013
MAIN MATERIALS: recycled cardboard
MAIN GREEN STRATEGIES: recycled materials

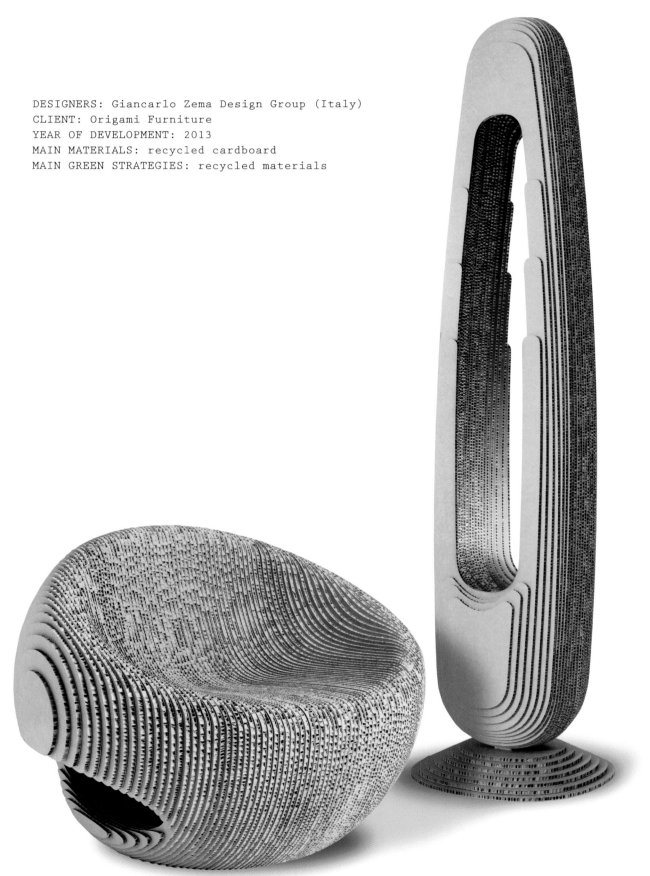

Mr. Cube

Mr. Cube is a collection of wooden figures with a common central body and interchangeable arms, legs, and head. The parts can be rearranged and offer a number of combination possibilities thanks to the internal magnets. When the toy is not in use, all the parts can be taken apart and rearranged to form a cube shape, which is much easier to store. The project was designed as part of 'Ten', an independent exhibition of personal responses to the concept of sustainable design by ten London-based designers.

Design: Héctor Serrano

DESIGNERS: Héctor Serrano (United Kingdom)
CLIENT: MUJI
YEAR OF DEVELOPMENT: 2011
MAIN MATERIALS: wood
MAIN GREEN STRATEGIES: sustainable materials

PHOTOS: COURTESY OF THE DESIGNERS

 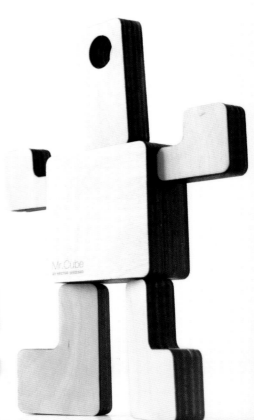

Bound Mirrors

The bespoke range of Bound Mirrors includes a number of different designs. Waterjet cut with hand-wrapped edges of hemp twine, the new range features a spectrum of new styles, materials and colors. The Bound hand mirror is refreshed in a version with hemp only along the handle. The Bound wall mirrors have also been transformed with the introduction of tinted mirrored glass - think bronze and grey - along with new hemp colors like bright pink and grass green.

Design:
Chelsea Green, James Minola

DESIGNERS: Chelsea Green, James Minola/Grain (USA)
DISTRIBUTOR: Grain
YEAR OF DEVELOPMENT: 2010
MAIN MATERIALS: mirrored clear glass,
FSC certified birch and hemp twine

PHOTOS: BEN BLOOD/WWW.BENBLOOD.COM

Tube Toys

Tube Toys are a series of vehicles to assemble where the packaging is also part of the product, considerably reducing the amount of material discarded after purchase, and the added cost that traditional packaging involves. All the parts needed to build each vehicle are contained in a standard cardboard tube, which doubles as the packaging and becomes the body of the car, fire engine, train or tractor. Each tube has pre-cut slots and holes to place the wheels axes and other components. A single stripe of paper displaying all the information needed, such as brand, logo, product name and barcode - is the only bit that will be discarded after purchase. All the materials used to create the product are also recycled and/or recyclable. The cars are easy to assemble and acknowledge the fact that children often enjoy playing with the packaging as much as with the actual toys.

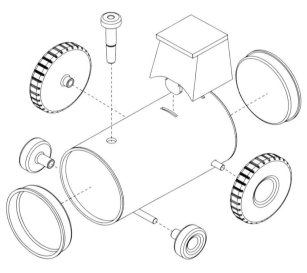

DESIGNERS: Óscar Diaz (United Kingdom)
CLIENT: NPW
YEAR OF DEVELOPMENT: 2012
MAIN MATERIALS: cardboard, rubber, bamboo, low-density polyethylene
MAIN GREEN STRATEGIES: recycled and recyclable materials

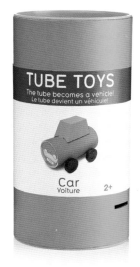

TUBE TOYS
The tube becomes a vehicle!
Le tube devient un véhicule!

Car
Voiture 2+

**Design:
Oscar Diaz**

TUBE TOYS
The tube becomes a vehicle!
Le tube devient un véhicule!

Fire Truck
Camion de Pompier 2+

TUBE TOYS
The tube becomes a vehicle!
Le tube devient un véhicule!

Train
Train 2+

Mixed

For this tableware prototype series
Studio Laurens van Wieringen mixed,
melted and produced their own material
from 580 kilograms of rejected plastic
from industries, toys and scrapyards
to create a brand new astonishing and
vibrant material. With every production,
the mixed and molten material leaves
a different and colorful print in the
product like a geological map. With this
combination Laurens van Wieringen created
an exciting range of products and objects
comprising various sizes of bowls, an
étagère, table plates, and cutlery.

DESIGNERS: Studio Laurens van Wieringen
(The Netherlands)
DISTRIBUTOR: Laurens van Wieringen
YEAR OF DEVELOPMENT: 2009
MAIN MATERIALS: recycled Polypropylene
MAIN GREEN STRATEGIES: recycled
materials, industrial waste

**Design: Laurens
van Wieringen**

Cantel

Van Eijk & Van der Lubbe designed the first collection of Imperfect Design. The products are developed together with different workshops in Guatamala. The result of this collaboration is a beautiful collection of ceramics, recycled-glass vases, and hand woven and embroidered plaids and cushions. The Cantel glass collection is made by local craftsmen in Guatemala and all items are hand-blown and made from recycled glass.

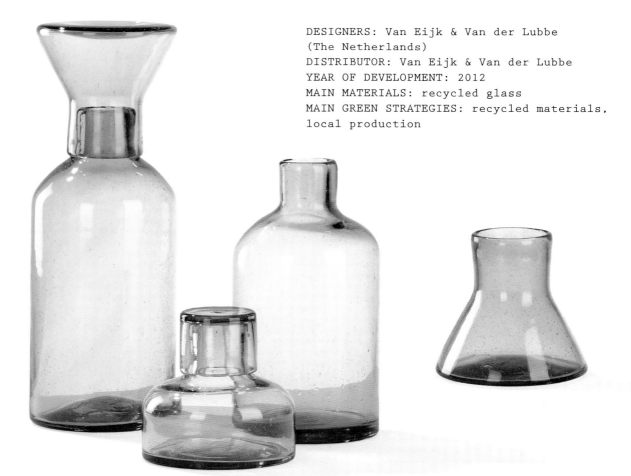

DESIGNERS: Van Eijk & Van der Lubbe (The Netherlands)
DISTRIBUTOR: Van Eijk & Van der Lubbe
YEAR OF DEVELOPMENT: 2012
MAIN MATERIALS: recycled glass
MAIN GREEN STRATEGIES: recycled materials, local production

**Design:
Miriam van der
Lubbe, Niels van
Eijk**

Eau Good

Over 22 billion plastic water bottles are discarded around the world every year. The designers wanted to reduce this waste by making tap water taste better in order to encourage people to stop buying bottled water. Binchotan charcoal has been used in Japan as a water purifier since the 17th century. It reduces chlorine, mineralizes the water and balances the pH. The designers designed a bottle which holds the raw charcaol in place without any additional components. The minimal design meant fewer parts to clean and it showed off the aesthetic beauty of the water and charcoal. Exposing the raw charcoal also meant that it could be recharged to extend its life.

DESIGNERS: black+blum (United Kingdom)
DISTRIBUTOR: black+blum
YEAR OF DEVELOPMENT: 2012
MAIN MATERIALS: copolyester (BPA free),
cork, silicon, stainless steel, Binchotan
charcoal
MAIN GREEN STRATEGIES: energy saving,
reusable, durable

PHOTOS: COURTESY OF THE DESIGNERS

**Design:
Dan Black, Martin Blum**

Seam

Seam is made of a specially engineered
woven polypropylene tailored in the shape
of a chair and a bench. Both are filled
with sand and then put in the oven under
pressure. After the baking process, the
sand is taken out, leaving a hollow,
super strong polypropylene structure.
Even the seams are polypropylene yarn.
This process also allows for high end
recycling. The project was made in
cooperation with Droog; the Aerospace
Engineering faculty of the Technical
University Delft; Composietenlab In-
holland Delft; and Lankhorst Indutech
in Sneek, the Netherlands.

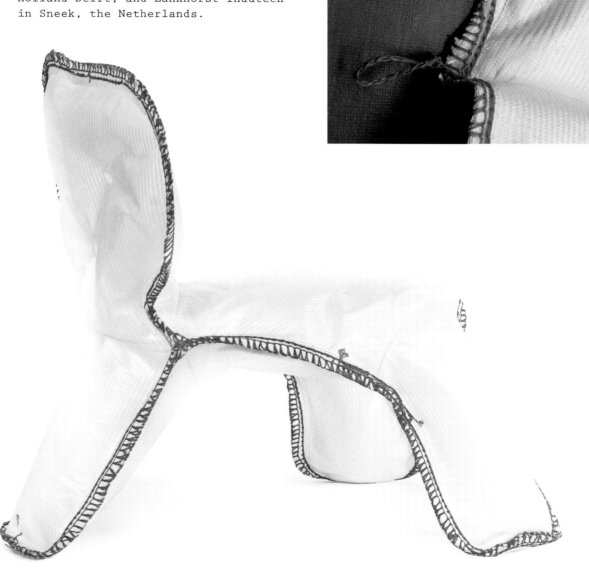

Design: Chris Kabel

DESIGNERS: Chris Kabel
(The Netherlands)
DISTRIBUTOR: Studio Chris Kabel
CLIENT: Drytech III by Droog
YEAR OF DEVELOPMENT: 2007
MAIN MATERIALS: polypropylene
MAIN GREEN STRATEGIES: recyclable,
low energy consumption, lightweight
construction

Recycled Wood Furniture

This range of furniture is made of reclaimed wood; painted, shaped by the weather and by many generations of people. Timeless, it is both old and new, originating from the past but looking to the future. The wood comes from a wide range of sources; old and broken houses, old wooden bridges, objects from the past. Mbiyen offers a kind of rare beauty, bridging the gap between past and present. That is the origin of Mbiyen, an Indonesian dialect word, which means the past or times gone by.

Design:
Krisna Mbiyen

DESIGNERS: Krisna Mbiyen (Indonesia)
YEAR OF DEVELOPMENT: 2010
MAIN MATERIALS: recycled teak wood, iron wood
MAIN GREEN STRATEGIES: recycled, highly durable, inherent natural beauty, modern design, exclusive products

Altrimenti

Altrimenti furniture provides proof of traditional craftsmanship techniques. The materials used and the work itself is both high quality. With a fine feel for aesthetic, each peace has been designed anew and decorated with historical ornamental patterns. Draws and interior spaces have been given a new and surprising colorful contrast. The result is unique pieces that bring a new character to modern living space. The company name stands for ecologically sustainable production and social engagement.

DESIGNERS: Patrizia Bernardinis, Daniel Schneider (Switzerland)
DISTRIBUTOR: Patrizia Bernardinis, Daniel Schneider
YEAR OF DEVELOPMENT: 2010
MAIN MATERIALS: wood, old furniture
MAIN GREEN STRATEGIES: local production, durable, upcycled furniture, sustainable, new life to old furniture, social engagement project

Design: Patrizia Bernardinis, Daniel Schneider

PHOTOS: WINFRIED HEINZE, FRANK BLASER, DANIEL SCHNEIDER, PORTRAIT: HEINER SCHMITT

Safe

Eliumstudio continues its research for Lexon on materials applied to mass-produced consumer products. This project involves the use of bio-plastic combined with bamboo on small consumer electronic devices and is a response to the growing environmental eco-conscience of present day design practices: the Safe line develops eco-engineered parts using totally renewable energies and materials.

DESIGNERS: Pierre Garner, Elise Berthier/ Eliumstudio (France)
DISTRIBUTOR: Lexon
YEAR OF DEVELOPMENT: 2011
MAIN MATERIALS: bamboo, bio-plastic
MAIN GREEN STRATEGIES: renewable materials, renewable energy

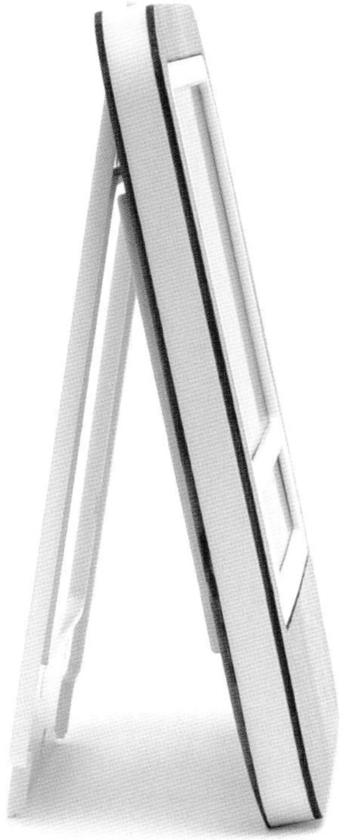

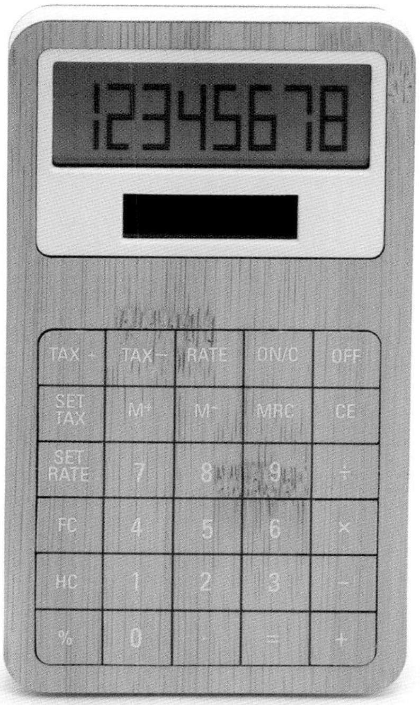

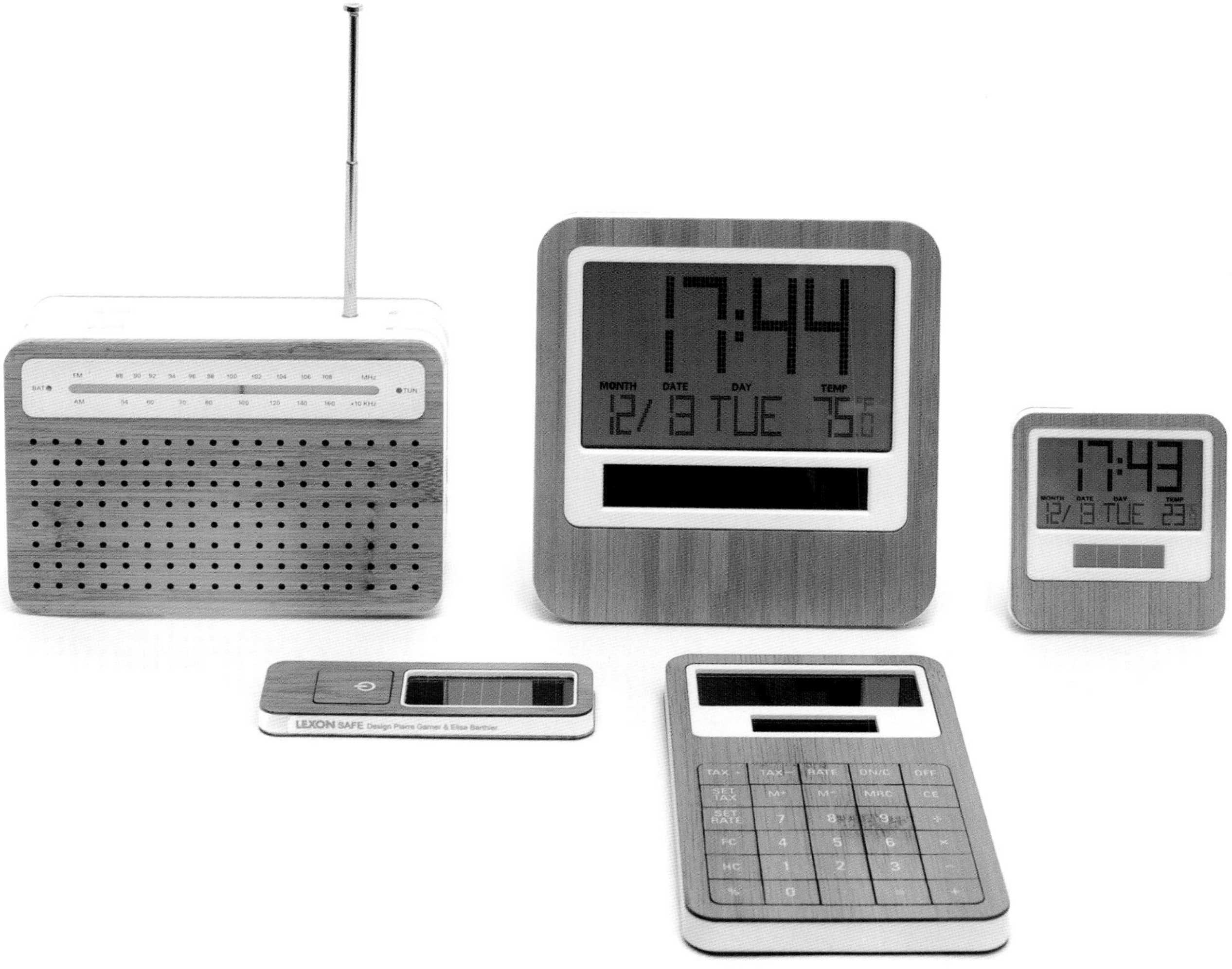

PHOTOS: COURTESY OF THE DESIGNERS

Eroded Stools

The eroded series was inspired by the natural process of erosion - where a solid material gets eaten away by an exogenic process. This not only results in changes to the quality of a solid object, but also leads to the formation of surfaces and pockets that then become suitable for different kinds of habitation. This concept is expressed by the product range, where the cork surface has been eroded to form an ergonomic seat or a storage pocket. Cork was chosen for its sustainable and environmentally friendly credentials. Sustainably sourced cork is harvested without damaging or cutting the tree. It is biodegradable and renewable, and has a low carbon footprint.

DESIGNERS: Alessandro Isola, Supriya Mankad/I M Lab (United Kingdom)
DISTRIBUTOR: I M Lab
YEAR OF DEVELOPMENT: 2013
MAIN MATERIALS: cork, wool felt
MAIN GREEN STRATEGIES: sustainable, environmentally friendly, biodegradable, renewable, low carbon footprint, sustainable materials, local production

Design: Alessandro Isola, Supriya Mankad

Bottle Cap Pouf and Bag

These products reuse bottle tops from all kinds of different bottles. Bottle tops come in a range of colors and sizes, an excellent raw material for creating vivid and colorful objects. Bottle tops are extremely difficult to recycle and yet they are still used to close all kinds of drinks bottles - millions are used and discarded every day. The stool and the bag were specially made for the Athens Green Design Festival 2008. The designer has also made a shopping trolley, jewelry and toys using this method. The process can be simplified and automated, making it easy for the customer to reuse the bottle tops themselves.

Design:
Athanasios Babalis

DESIGNERS: Athanasios Babalis (Greece)
DISTRIBUTOR: Athanasios Babalis
YEAR OF DEVELOPMENT: 2008
MAIN MATERIALS: recycled bottle cups,
fishing line
MAIN GREEN STRATEGIES: recycled
materials, re-use, local production,
sustainable design

PHOTOS: ANGELOS ZYMARAS, PORTRAIT: EMMANOUIL PAPADOPOULOS

Combine Line

All tableware in this range is made from
ecologically responsible and certified
materials. The unique products are
created with a mixture of bambootube
and a moldable biodegradable substance
comprising bamboo fibers and rice hulls.
Available in 11 colors, the complete
set comprises two large bowls, a bowl
with compartments for finger food, a
saucepot, plates, cups and coasters.
The set can be bought as a whole or in
parts.

DESIGNERS: Leo Eyer & Bold_a design company team (Brazil)
DISTRIBUTOR: Bold_a design company
YEAR OF DEVELOPMENT: 2013
MAIN MATERIALS: bambootube, moldable biodegradable
substance including bamboo fibers, rice hulls
MAIN GREEN STRATEGIES: sustainable materials

**Design:
Leonardo Eyer**

Growth Series

Growth Series is a collection of ceramic vases combined with natural twigs. It is a group of vessels that juxtaposes the natural found elements with the handmade stoneware body. The designer uses local and recycled materials to create the vases and this combined with low energy production techniques and the use of found materials makes this an elegant and environmentally friendly product range.

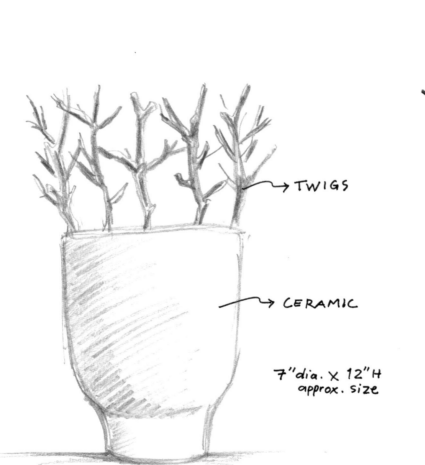

→ TWIGS

→ CERAMIC

7"dia. X 12"H approx. size

DESIGNERS: Stanley Ruiz (USA)
DISTRIBUTOR: Stanley Ruiz
YEAR OF DEVELOPMENT: 2009
MAIN MATERIALS: stoneware, natural twigs
MAIN GREEN STRATEGIES: handmade, local production, recycled materials, found materials, low energy production

Design:
Stanley Ruiz

PHOTOS: STANLEY RUIZ, PORTRAIT: DALE JABAGAT

Light

The subject of providing artificial lighting gives designers the opportunity to showcase inventive green design ideas. Where, if not here, can one show that a responsible use of natural resources does not mean that beauty and style have to be foresaken. Energy saving lamps and LEDs cater to the technical demands of modern, environmentally friendly living and are extensively used in today's society. Solar energy is already frequently used: sunlight is stored as energy in rechargeable batteries and then released as artificial light. This creates an independent light-store, which charges during the day and later, lights up the night. Conventional green production processes do, however, also play an important role: Designers deliberate over which materials are sustainable, what can be reused, ecologically responsible forms of transport and packaging and even eco friendly glue, threads etc. Lampshades have been created from recycled materials, old obsolete objects and even industrial waste. The resulting products are individual and often do not in any way resemble the original product as the change of function is so radical. The 'waste' material begins a second life that has functionally nothing to do with the first. Many of the designs displayed in this chapter are truly light sculptures, influenced by earlier, classical

forms of lighting such as the chande-
lier. Others, like the Lamponi Lamps,
preserve the charme of the old product -
a Vespa for example - in their new function. These models allow older styles an
elegant new life, demonstrating what the
right use of energy and resources can
look like.

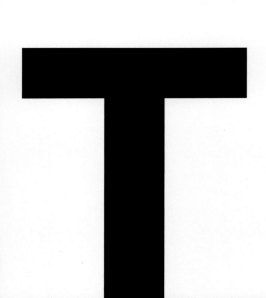

NanoLeaf

This LED bulb produces an impressive 133 lumens per watt, with no heatsink - an unprecedented achievement for LED bulbs. The high lumens output far surpasses the 93.4 lumens per watt produced by last year's US Department of Energy winner for energy efficient lighting. NanoLeaf promises a lifespan of about 30,000 hours. The LEDs are directly attached to the printed circuit board (PCB) and folded into its unique shape. This somewhat unconventional design maximizes energy efficiency to reduce heat output, and creates an omnidirectional bulb which enables an even distribution of light in all directions.

**Design:
Gimmy Chu,
Tom Rodinger,
Christian Yan**

DESIGNERS: Tom Rodinger, Gimmy Chu,
Christian Yan/NanoLeaf (China/USA)
DISTRIBUTOR: NanoGrid Ltd.
YEAR OF DEVELOPMENT: 2013
MAIN MATERIALS: printed circuit board
MAIN GREEN STRATEGIES: energy
efficient, contains no mercury

Bipolar Pendant Lights

The Bipolar pendant light is part of the In Vitro Collection, which pays tribute to the beauty and the eclecticism of the glassware industry. Each product is carefully handmade in Montreal, Canada with upcycled glass items from donations or local community-run second-hand shops. The Bipolar is created from two wine glasses or champagne flutes without their base. An anodized aluminum ring wraps a strip of LED lights in the middle. Although long-lasting and energy efficient, the LEDs can be removed and replaced by unscrewing the top of the ring. The lamps come in diverse shapes, colors and sizes and the original bases are used to make spinning tops or yoyos; nothing is wasted. In Vitro is the rebirth of the rejected, the out of style, and the damaged.

Design: Tat Chao

DESIGNERS: Tat Chao
DISTRIBUTOR: Tat Chao
YEAR OF DEVELOPMENT: 2012
MAIN MATERIALS: upcycled glassware, anodized aluminum
MAIN GREEN STRATEGIES: up-cycled material, local material, hand made production, low energy consumption, local production

Glowworm

In spite of the short winter days and long nights, the sun is still the most powerful source of energy for mankind. The only energy source Glowworm requires is the sun. The lamp can be used as a table or floor lamp, or it can be located in open space. Photovoltaic cells are located on the outside of the three adjustable arms. The user can alter the shape of the lamp according to their mood or needs. The whole concept is inspired by the worm Lampyris noctiluca, which is known for its ability to glow in the dark. Just like living creatures need sunlight to survive, the Glowworm needs the sun in order to shine.

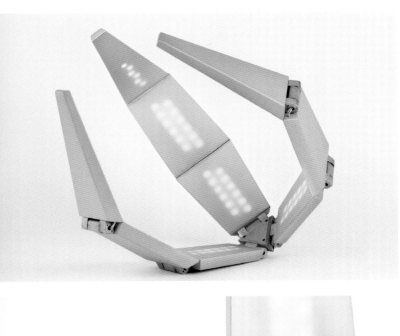
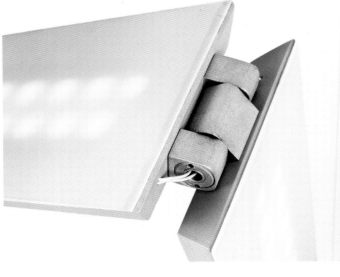
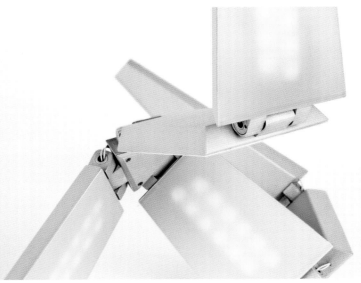
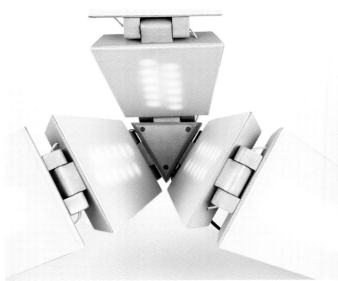

DESIGNERS: Lenka Czereova (Slovakia)
YEAR OF DEVELOPMENT: 2008
MAIN MATERIALS: dural, aluminum, LED
MAIN GREEN STRATEGIES: low energy
consumption

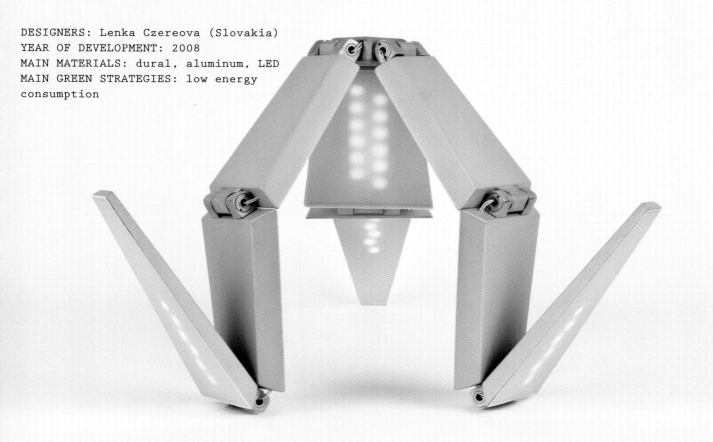

PHOTOS: ALLT. PORTRAIT: COURTESY BY THE DESIGNER

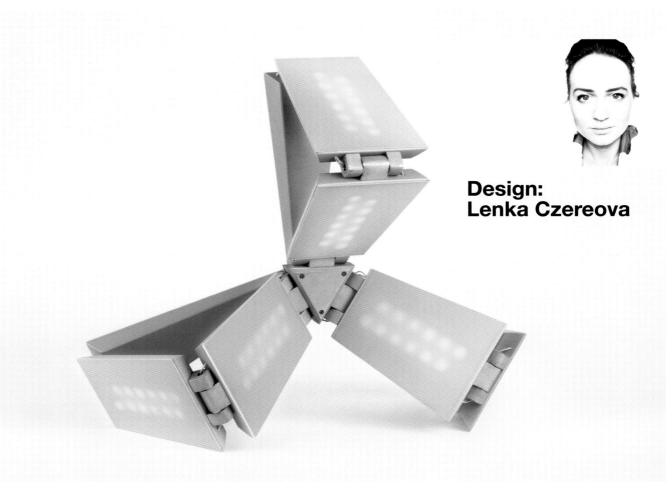

**Design:
Lenka Czereova**

Eistla

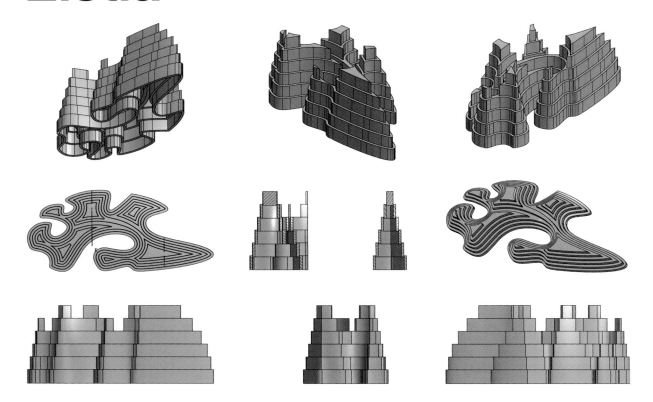

Stephen Shaheen's Eistla series comprises dynamic, sculptural furnishings made from onyx. Cut to a width of one centimeter, Eistla is a versatile product that can be suspended from the ceiling, placed on the floor as a stalagmite luminaire, or even used as a table base. To avoid wastefully carving an entire block of stone, Shaheen designed Eistla to be crafted from small onyx cutoffs that are laminated and cut with advanced technologies to produce volumetric forms. These are lightweight and emphasize the natural character and beauty of this translucent stone. The pieces are illuminated with energy-efficient LEDs.

Design: Stephen Shaheen

DESIGNERS: Stephen Shaheen (USA)
DISTRIBUTOR: Stephen Shaheen Studios
YEAR OF DEVELOPMENT: 2011
MAIN MATERIALS: onyx
MAIN GREEN STRATEGIES: recycled/salvaged materials, minimization of
waste, low energy consumption

Crush Lamps

Design: Vanessa Battaglia, Brendan Young

The Big Crush floor lamp and Little Crush table lamp are made of crushed plastic drink bottles, shaped to form a sculptural lamp base. The interesting design promotes upcycling practices, encouraging consumers to take another look at what at first glance appears to be just rubbish and to think about how rubbish can be put to good use. The lamps come in a range of colors, including red, gold, and black and were on display during London Design Week.

DESIGNERS: Vanessa Battaglia, Brendan Young/
Studiomold (United Kingdom)
YEAR OF DEVELOPMENT: 2007
MAIN MATERIALS: crushed plastic drinks
bottles
MAIN GREEN STRATEGIES: upcycling practice

PHOTOS: STUDIOMOLD

VickyLamp

A lamp is one of the most appreciated elements in the household. It is a vitally important source of light and makes our daily routines easier. What if a lamp was not only a light source, but also a resource that could be used to grow food? Nowadays, households in the bigger cities are surrounded by higher buildings and in the worst case by skyscrapers. These buildings block valuable sunlight from entering houses and apartments. The designer has come up with an idea to solve this problem. This Victorian lamp uses a special light that provides an increased radiation on the blue spectrum. Thanks to Vicky lamp you can enjoy planting small edible plants or simply enjoy nature in places, which lack natural light.

DESIGNERS: José Rodrigo de la O Campos (Mexico)
YEAR OF DEVELOPMENT: 2012
MAIN MATERIALS: copper, wood, silicone
MAIN GREEN STRATEGIES: promotes urban gardening

**Design:
José Rodrigo de la
O Campos**

PHOTOS: JOSÉ DE LA O CAMPOS, ALEJANDRO CABRERA, MAGA STUDIOS MEXICO

Lamponi Lamps

This diverse range of lamps is made from recycled motorcycle parts and is perfect for anyone interested in motorbike or retro design. The lamps are made by Italian artist Maurizio Lamponi Leopardi and give any space a unique and stylish character. The lamps are made from a wide selection of parts and colors so that each piece is unique.

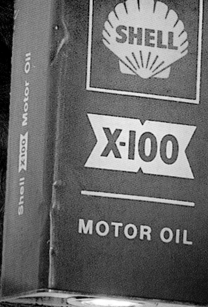

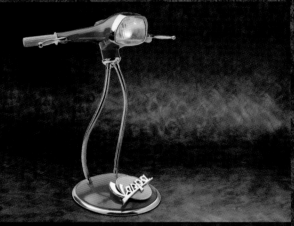

DESIGNERS: Maurizio Lamponi Leopardi (Italy)
YEAR OF DEVELOPMENT: 1988-2013
MAIN MATERIALS: recycled motocycle parts
MAIN GREEN STRATEGIES: use of recycled materials

**Design: Maurizio
Lamponi Leopardi**

Utrem Lux

At Degross Studio the designers focus on efficiency, maximizing the use of raw materials and minimizing waste. When the designers found a bin full of glass bottles discarded behind their studio, they decided to try and use them. They experimented with the glass until they found a way to split it without breaking it. They then combined the old glass bottles with wood offcuts donated by a nearby timber yard. The outcome of this experimental process was the Utrem Lux, a range of lamps made from up-cycled glass bottles and wood offcuts. The range was first launched during the London Design Week in September 2012.

Design: Alon Gross

PHOTOS: ALEXANDER DUFFNER. PORTRAIT: SABRINA GROSS

DESIGNERS: Degross design and Innovation
(United Kingdom)
DISTRIBUTOR: Degross design and Innovation
YEAR OF DEVELOPMENT: 2012
MAIN MATERIALS: sapele wood, reused amber
glass bottles
MAIN GREEN STRATEGIES: recycled materials

WesternTrash

WesternTrash is designer lighting
and glassware with Berlin soul. The
designers make high-quality items from
recycled bottles. Creating something
from nothing, they challenge people
to think differently about discarded
objects. The intention of the project
is to create quality glassware while
addressing the problems of landfill and
pollution. The products are handcrafted,
meaning that no two are the same. Each

one is an individual work of art,
inspired by the creative energy of
Berlin. WesternTrash is sustainable;
100 percent recycled materials, no
waste, and locally sourced materials.

DESIGNERS: Krzysztof Zielinski (Germany)
YEAR OF DEVELOPMENT: 2011
MAIN MATERIALS: glass
MAIN GREEN STRATEGIES: recycled materials,
recyclable, local production, durable, low
energy consumption

**Design:
Western Trash**

Ignite Lamp

Design: Colleen Jordan

The Ignite Lamp is a lamp that reacts to the world around it. It is made from a combination of recycled and new materials. The lamp is solar powered, charging two small batteries that power the light. The circuit inside includes a microphone that takes the input of the sound around it, and translates it to output, increasing the brightness of the lamp. As the sound around the lamp increases, the brightness of the lamp increases as well.

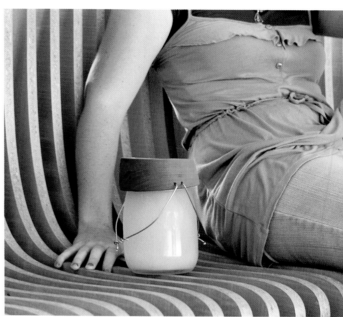

DESIGNERS: Colleen Jordan (USA)
YEAR OF DEVELOPMENT: 2013
MAIN MATERIALS: recycled glass, LED, solar
panels, rechargeable batteries, wood,
recycled bike spoke
MAIN GREEN STRATEGIES: recycled materials,
low energy, solar power, material reuse

The Quality of Mercy

The Quality of Mercy is a five-meter-long suspended sculpture made from 1,000 plastic bottles cleaned up from rivers in Columbus, Ohio. It uses solar powered fiber optics to illuminate and shift gradually in color temperature once the sun goes down. The Quality of Mercy was created while the artist was in residence at the Franklin Park Conservatory and Botanical Gardens in conjunction with her exhibit Sacrifice + Bliss in 2012/13. The conservatory and the artist invested in the creation of this piece in order to raise awareness about plastic pollution and help clean up our most valuable shared resource, water. Proceeds from the sale of this work will go to continue cleaning up rivers, oceans and waterways.

DESIGNERS: Aurora Robson for Project Vortex (USA)
DISTRIBUTOR: Aurora Robson/Project Vortex
YEAR OF DEVELOPMENT: 2012
MAIN MATERIALS: polyethylene terephthalate, (plastic debris/pollution), solar powered fiber optics
MAIN GREEN STRATEGIES: intercepting the waste stream

ilumi

Design: ilumi

Ilumi brings energy efficient lighting to life giving you full wireless control to tune, program, and automate the color and brightness of your lighting all through a convenient mobile app. The patent pending series of Bluetooth enabled multicolor LED lights create amazing lighting experiences, pay for themselves in energy savings, and give you an advanced lighting control system that is as easy as changing a light bulb. Ilumi is currently available in two sizes, a large PAR30 and a small A21. With complete flexibility of color and robust wireless control and programming, ilumi is perfect for the home or commercial locations such as restaurants, hotels, bars, event spaces, offices, and wellness centers. The vast array of lighting experiences include a simulated sunrise, circadian rhythm lighting, music sync lighting, vacation security, proximity lighting, and much more.

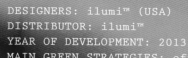

DESIGNERS: ilumi™ (USA)
DISTRIBUTOR: ilumi™
YEAR OF DEVELOPMENT: 2013
MAIN GREEN STRATEGIES: efficient LEDs and
lighting automation, each ilumi is RoHS
compliant and lasts up to 20 years

PHOTOS: MATT EGAN

Merry-Go-Round

Merry-Go-Round uses industrial waste material from local companies to create products, which make optimal use of a material's inherent characteristics. The variation in resources is the starting point of the design process, following through all the way to the final product. This project arose as the result of a collaboration between design collective Design Stories and producers and artisans Returhuset. The designers also work with local producers, who give them their waste.

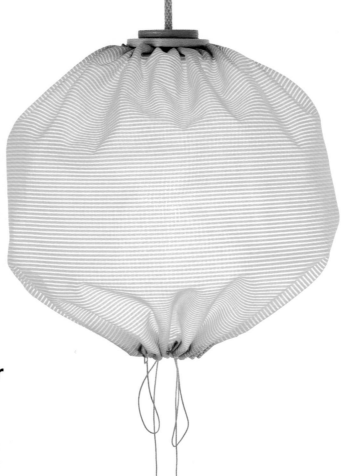

Design:
Kerstin Sylwan,
Sara Danielsson,
Jenny Stefansdotter

PHOTOS: HENDRIK ZEITLER, PORTRAIT: ILAR GUNILLA PERSSON

DESIGNERS: Kerstin Sylwan, Sara Danielsson, Jenny Stefansdotter/
Design Stories (Sweden)
DISTRIBUTOR: Design Stories/Returhuset
YEAR OF DEVELOPMENT: 2012
MAIN MATERIALS: textile, wood, electrical components
MAIN GREEN STRATEGIES: reused textile waste, local production,
low energy consumption, durable, social production

PassaCabos

PassaCabos cork is an innovative design that uses ecological and traditional material. The project aims to explore the relationship between objects and animals, and humans in everyday life. The designer was inspired by a story about ferrets, which were trained to pass electrical cables inside ducts. Portuguese cork was chosen as the main material because it is 100 percent natural, biodegradable, and thus very environmentally friendly.

Design:
André Valério

DESIGNERS: André Valério (Portugal)
DISTRIBUTOR: Ervilha Criativa, Lda
YEAR OF DEVELOPMENT: 2011
MAIN MATERIALS: cork, linen cord-set
MAIN GREEN STRATEGIES: recyclable,
sustainable materials, local production

PHOTOS: RAQUEL ABREU, SÍLVIA DUARTE, PORTRAIT: EDUARDA ABRANTES

Candles Decafé

These simple yet elegant candle holders are organically made from decafé, a new patented material made from used coffee grounds. The project is intended to provoke thought and discussions about everyday waste. Coffee grounds were the perfect material as they are easily recognizable and available in great quantities. The new material is the result of a long experimentation process, patience and dedication. The products are completely handmade. Coffee grounds are mixed with a natural binding substance and then subjecting them to a pressurizing process.

**Design:
Raúl Laurí Pla**

DESIGNERS: Raúl Laurí Pla (Spain)
DISTRIBUTOR: Raúl Laurí design lab
YEAR OF DEVELOPMENT: 2013
MAIN MATERIALS: decafé (new
material extracted from used
coffee grounds)
MAIN GREEN STRATEGIES: recycled,
hand-craft, sustainable,
simplicity, essence, profitable
wastes, local resources,
sustainable materials, local
production

Public

This chapter is dedicated to green design in public space and shows examples of how street furniture can contribute to a better environment. It concerns itself particularly with motion - with a bike, motorized scooter or car. Countless designers have focused their attention on developing ways of making transportation environmentally friendly. Bike designs have been reduced to just the bare essentials, making them lighter and often collapsible in form. These designs are becoming more widely available, which has resulted in more people using them.

Bikes and scooters with an electrical motor are also being aimed at a wider market. Although these use more energy than a traditional pedal-bike, they are considerably more 'green' than their petrol guzzling counter-parts. Obviously, when it comes to electricpowered transportation there is some discrepancy in the efficiency of different versions. The more compact designs presents - in crowded inner-cities with heavy traffic a significant 'green' factor - whether in stationary or moving traffic. More often, as with the other products included

in this book, designers have to pay attention to the whether the energy source
is renweable or not. Besides the e-Cars
and bikes there are now solar planes
and boats. Electric vehicles should be
"hip", stripped back and clearly modern,
appealing to a diverse and open-minded
consumer group to allow their accep-
tance and use to be increased, currently the greatest innovations appeal
to groups who are also experimenters and
Early Adopters. Not taken into account
here, are the current models from promi-
nent manufacturers, who can or must come

up with a new product every six months,
that tackles issues of environmental
impact. The ecological correctness of a
car has become an important success-fac-
tor and an influential advertising slo-
gan, but the steps taken here are small,
largely because novation not innovation
is the deciding factor.

BLIC

Solar Impulse

In 2003 a visionary and an entrepreneur, Bertrand Piccard and André Borschberg, launched a project to develop the world's first solar airplane capable of flying day and night. Seven years later, in 2010, their vision became reality: Solar Impulse's HB-SIA prototype succeeded in flying 26 hours powered by nothing but solar energy. Building the aircraft required the optimization of new and existing technologies while pushing the limits for a drastic reduction in energy consumption. It's a scientific and innovative initiative while also acting as a messenger: through innovation, and without reducing economic growth and mobility, new energy sources can be found. A second-generation airplane is currently under construction and will undertake the unprecedented challenge of completing a strictly solar-powered round-the-world tour in 2015.

**Design:
André Borschberg and
Bertrand Piccard**

DESIGNERS: Solar Impulse Team, coordinated by Bertrand Piccard and André
Borschberg (Switzerland)
DISTRIBUTOR: Solar Impulse
YEAR OF DEVELOPMENT: 2003-2010
MAIN MATERIALS: carbon fiber, solar cells, 4 lithium-ion batteries,
brushless electric motors, specialized polymers
MAIN GREEN STRATEGIES: first to fly day and night only on solar power,
energy efficiency, technological innovation, engineering excellence,
sustainable future

New London Bus

This innovative new bus concept is a brand new London classic that retains the much loved friendly and warm feeling of the Routemaster. A compact bus for a compact city: it is shorter than the original and has a small wheelbase, which means it can move easily around London's narrow streets. One of the most characteristic features is the diagonal window that visually enhances the stairs, which are an integral part of the Routemaster's iconic design.

To improve safety, the designers have incorporated a lighting system into the floor of the rear entrance platform that informs passengers and vehicles when the bus is about to depart. This is a truly sustainable vehicle using a hybrid diesel-electric drive system. The reduced size also results in less fuel consumption and fewer emissions.

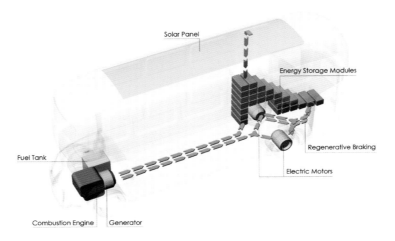

DESIGNERS: Héctor Serrano Studio,
Miñarro García and Javier Esteban
(United Kingdom)
DISTRIBUTOR: prototype
YEAR OF DEVELOPMENT: 2011
MAIN GREEN STRATEGIES: hybrid diesel-
electric drive system, reduced fuel
consumption

Wood Bicycle

These wooden bikes are made using old woodworking joinery with no fasteners just good glue and joinery techniques. The wooden Bicycles are constructed using a combination of hardwoods and multi-ply wood. Using handmade templates, the designers cut out the shapes for the bikes and then hand file them smooth to the right shape. They then mark out needed holes for dropouts, bottom brackets, headtube etc. before cutting the dowels needed. This is followed by more handwork to complete the joins for the head tube and the forks. Lastly, the parts are then fitted together and tested. The bikes are then finished with a rubbed oil finish.

Design: Bill Holloway, Mauro Hernandez

DESIGNERS: Bill Holloway, Mauro Hernandez/Masterworks Wood and Design (USA)
DISTRIBUTOR: Masterworks Wood and Design
YEAR OF DEVELOPMENT: 2010
MAIN MATERIALS: urban woods, multiply woods, hardwoods
MAIN GREEN STRATEGIES: urban wood, reused materials, environmentally safe
finishes, durable, local production

Moveo

Moveo is a foldable electric scooter, intended to revolutionize urban traffic and commuting by meeting ever-increasing needs for personal mobility. The scooter can be stored easily, used either as an individual or a last-mile transport solution and requires no parking space. Moveo can travel up to 45 km/h and cover a distance of 35 km with one single charge. Its low consumption of 2 kWh/100 km makes it an economic individual transport. It can be folded and pulled along, while the seat becomes a backpack. The lightweight carbon-composite body weighs just 25 kilograms and the two-wheel drive gives extraordinary driving comfort. Other features include a leather seat with backrest, disk brakes, and LED lights.

DESIGNERS: Peter Uveges/Moveo (Hungary)
DISTRIBUTOR: Moveo Co.
YEAR OF DEVELOPMENT: 2011
MAIN MATERIALS: carbon fiber reinforced composite body; CNC/cast aluminum
MAIN GREEN STRATEGIES: low energy consumption enabled by ultra light weight, recuperative braking, local production, manual assembly, durable, recyclable materials

Design:
Peter Uveges

RETO

These unique surfboards are created from old skateboards. Skateboarding evolved from surfing in the late 1950s and this is a way of giving something back to surfing. The designer began collecting old skateboards from all over Finland and as the design concept began to take shape, he started researching how surfboards were built during the 1970s, when they were still made of wood - unlike modern boards that are made of polystyrene foam covered in layers of fiberglass. The research phase was followed by months of experimenting and the final design is similar to a puzzle, made up of hundreds of small pieces slotted together. The boards are hollow to make them as light as possible.

DESIGNERS: Björn Holm (Finland)
DISTRIBUTOR: Björn Holm
YEAR OF DEVELOPMENT: 2012
MAIN MATERIALS: broken skateboard decks
MAIN GREEN STRATEGIES: recycling, use of sustainable materials

Design: Björn Holm

Portable Water Generator

This project is the result of a collaboration between Peruvian researchers and an advertising agency. Lima receives less than three centimeters of rainfall each year. Despite this, the high humidity makes it possible to harvest water directly from the air. The large billboard generates drinking water from humid air. The billboard serves as a traditional advertising devise while simultaneously collecting moisture directly from the air. The water is then cleaned by means of a filtration system. The system is capable of producing 96 liters of water each day.

DESIGNERS: Mayo DraftFbc (Peru)
YEAR OF DEVELOPMENT: 2012
MAIN MATERIALS: UV lamps, filters
MAIN GREEN STRATEGIES: condensation of atmospheric water, water purification

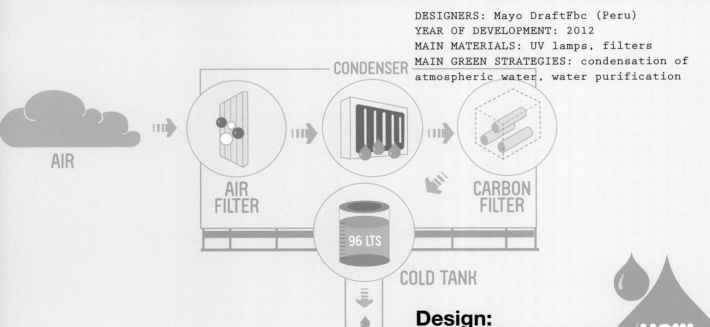

AIR

AIR FILTER

CONDENSER

CARBON FILTER

96 LTS

COLD TANK

**Design:
Alejandro Aponte, Humberto Polar, Juan Donalisio**

HOW IT WORKS

Biolamp

Design: Peter Horvath

This elegant biolamp is design to purify the air. The designer chose to create a streetlamp, as this is a common object, found everywhere. The lamps contain liquid algae mixed with water, which converts carbon dioxide to oxygen. The upper part of the lamp functions as a ventilator, drawing polluted air in from the outside. This is then circulated inside the lamp to allow for effective absorption of carbon dioxide. The combination of sunlight, carbon dioxide and water transforms the algae into biomass. This is a waste product that can be used as fuel, giving the lamps a dual purpose as both air cleaners and fuel providers. After the saturated biomass has been removed, the lamps can be refilled with algae and the process starts all over again.

DESIGNERS: Biolamp (Hungary)
YEAR OF DEVELOPMENT: 2010
MAIN MATERIALS: aluminum, glass, algae liquid
MAIN GREEN STRATEGIES: the object is designed aimed air cleaning and the production of fuel

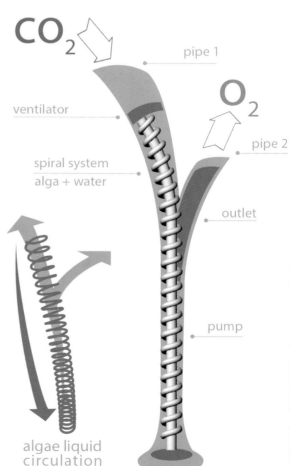

Casple Podadera City Car

This two-person city car was developed
as a collaboration between Spanish
designers Casple and Francisco Podadera.
The tiny eco-friendly vehicle can be
folded, so that it takes up as little
as just two meters parking space. The
car's robust tubular structure comprises
composite materials and honeycomb
panels, meeting side-impact safety
criteria. The car can travel up to 130
kilometers on one battery charge, and
reaches a top speed of 110 kilometers
per hour.

PHOTOS: FRANCISCO PODADERA

DESIGNERS: Francisco Podadera (Spain)
DISTRIBUTOR: prototype
YEAR OF DEVELOPMENT: 2013
MAIN MATERIALS: tubular chassis and RTM
composites bodywork
MAIN GREEN STRATEGIES: electric vehicle

K-abeilles

One outside wall of this hut is made of compartments shaped like alveoli. These small shelters are filled with various materials, such as bricks, twigs, reeds, bark, hay etc. The densely packed materials create ideal habitats for wild bees. The internal space is a shelter for people, made of wood and fitted with wooden furniture that carries on the theme of a beehive. Some of the hexagonal compartments in the hut walls have been left open, blurring the boundary between inside and outside.

DESIGNERS: Atelierd.Org (France)
DISTRIBUTOR: Atelierd.Org
YEAR OF DEVELOPMENT: 2012
MAIN MATERIALS: wood (spruce), natural filling for bees (branches, rolled up braids of reeds, hollow bricks)

Design: Atelierd.Org

Solowheel

The Solowheel is a small, green and convenient mode of transportation. This gyro-stabilized electric unicycle is compact and fun to ride and can be used like an electric bicycle. Weighing 12 kilos, the Solowheel was designed to be lightweight and easy to use. It can be taken to the office, classroom, restaurant, or on the bus or train. The built-in carrying handle makes it easy to quickly pick up when you get to a flight of stairs. With the foot pedals folded up, it takes up no more space than a briefcase. Using a Solowheel instead of a car reduces gas costs, pollution, and traffic. Riders with short commutes can travel to work or school on the Solowheel, charge the unit in the office or classroom, and ride back home.

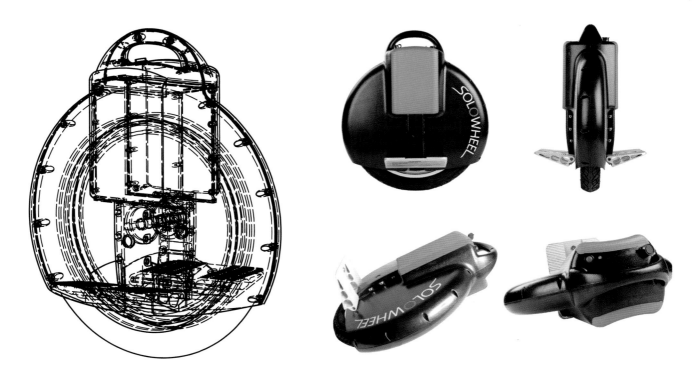

DESIGNERS: Shane Chen (USA)
YEAR OF DEVELOPMENT: 2011
MAIN MATERIALS: aluminum, steel, plastic
MAIN GREEN STRATEGIES:electric non-polluting transportation

PHOTOS: KARLI RIZZO, SHANE CHEN, ALEX ROE, DARREN KORMANDY, RICH SERRA

Design: Shane Chen

Lotus E-bike

This is an innovative, sustainable, pedal-assisted, sophisticated electric bike. The main aluminum structure is just one single curve that starts at the front of the bike and incorporates the pedals before enveloping the back wheel. The design conceals the integrated battery and the brushless BionX electric motor, which ends below the comfortable saddle. The maintenance-free shaft transmits pedaling power accurately and silently. The large LED touch screen display also gives information on charge status, road systems and conditions and the nearest Lotus recharging points. An ergonomic shape and practical storage containers complete the highly intuitive and comfortable system.

**Design:
Giancarlo Zema**

DESIGNERS: Giancarlo Zema Design Group (Italy)
DISTRIBUTOR: LumineXence
YEAR OF DEVELOPMENT: 2012
MAIN MATERIALS: aluminum
MAIN GREEN STRATEGIES: recycling, use of durable
materials

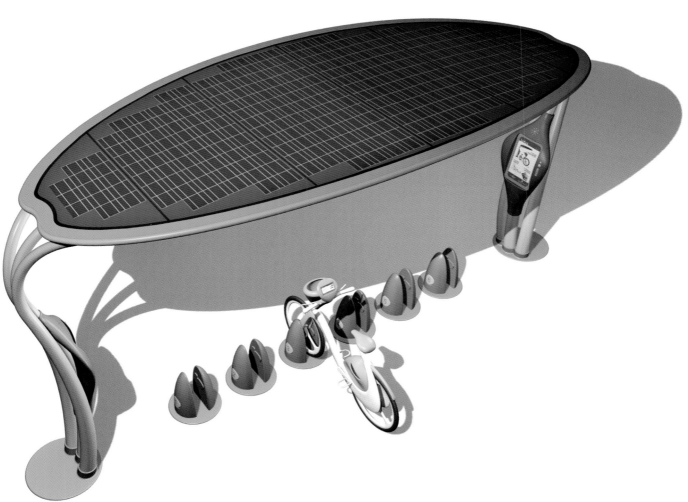

SolarSails

Design: Robert Dane

This innovative design utilizes sun and wind power, combined with a sophisticated computer system, to power a large boat. Designer Robert Dane began investigating the implementation of hybrid marine power and the use of solar sails in all branches of the marine industry. Solar sailing significantly cuts fuel costs and lowers a ship's environmental impact. The technology can be used on all kinds of boats, from small vessels to bulk carriers.

DESIGNERS: Robert Dane (Australia)
DISTRIBUTOR: SolarSailor
YEAR OF DEVELOPMENT: 2013
MAIN MATERIALS: lightweight marine materials
MAIN GREEN STRATEGIES: low energy consumption, 50% fuel reduction

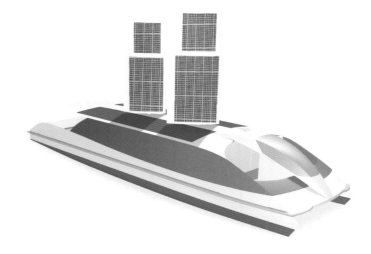

PHOTOS: SOLARSAILOR

Thonet Concept Bike

At the end of 2010 London based designer Andy Martin was asked by Thonet to design and develop ideas for a concept bicycle using their steam bending process developed in the 1930s. Martin studio created three different designs and selected the 'fixed wheel' to develop for its simplicity and beauty. The main challenge faced by the designer, was taking on the fairly low

tech process of steam bending and then applying it to a 21st century bicycle with highly complex engineering. With the many restrictions of hand bending the beech frame, the final jointing and contours must be cut and adjusted on a CNC machine. Andy Martin has also developed a series of connectors and sprung rods to reinforce joints and the major stress areas in the frame.

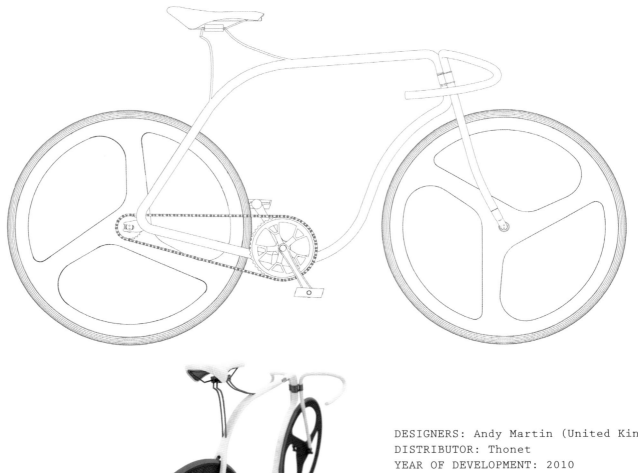

DESIGNERS: Andy Martin (United Kingdom)
DISTRIBUTOR: Thonet
YEAR OF DEVELOPMENT: 2010
MAIN MATERIALS: cork, linen cord-set
MAIN GREEN STRATEGIES: low tech process
steam bending

**Design:
Andy Martin**

Coboc 3.0

The Coboc eCycle is a "Pedelec" - a
bicycle with an electric motor. Its
special features are its minimalism, its
low weight and its intuitive handling.
The total weight of the current prototype
is 13.9 kilograms. All components of
the drive train are integrated in the
Coboc's frame. The design concept has
been stripped back to the essentials;
it is operated by the rider's muscle
power, reacting directly to the rider's
impulses. Optimizing this process was a
key focus of the design process.

Design: David Horsch,
Pius Warken

DESIGNERS: David Horsch, Pius Warken, COBOC eCycles
(Germany)
YEAR OF DEVELOPMENT: 2012
MAIN MATERIALS: ALLOY AI 7020
MAIN GREEN STRATEGIES: local production of the entire
frame, e-mobility, durable, repairable battery

PHOTOS: COURTESY OF THE DESIGNERS

Kenguru

The Kenguru is a 100 percent electrically powered vehicle that is purpose built for people in wheelchairs. With the Kenguru, a wheelchair user is no longer trapped in one place or dependent on others. They can now travel up to nearly 100 kilometers a day at 40 kmh. The Kenguru is very easy to use, allowing drivers to enter at the push of a button, and to drive while seated in their own wheelchair. The Kenguru is capable of changing the mobility of disabled people for the better.

DESIGNERS: Community Cars, Inc.(USA)
DISTRIBUTOR: Community Cars, Inc.
YEAR OF DEVELOPMENT: 2012
MAIN MATERIALS: steel chassis, fiberglass body, electric motors and 12 volt batteries
MAIN GREEN STRATEGIES: 100% electric vehicle

Work

In the private sector, the use of green products depends on two major factors: economic efficiency and reputation. Because of this, products in this area have a particularly good chance of success if they are good value for money or well reputed. So, energy-saving products that can be used in offices hold all of the cards. Allowing green products to have an economical advantage is often a matter of legislative will. Thus, products that are not 'green', can be encumbered with costs resulting from their production practices or recycled plastic can be funded, to the extent to which new plastic with no recycled content is burdened with extra taxes and costs. Working together with these control mechanisms though, is the product composition itself, which can bring a product a financial advantage: efficient composition, durability - or products with a short life-span, when desired, with uncomplicated recycling options - and reduced energy usage are properties that the designer can bring to the object. It can even be something as simple as the engineer and designer work closely together with the available technical equipment. Both are then engaged with bringing the

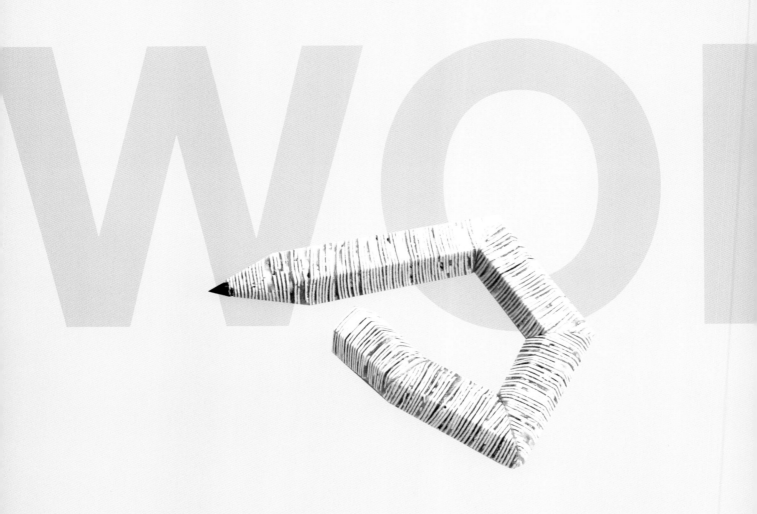

latest technological innovation to the new product and therefore keep up to date with new research. Products that are strongly dependent upon current research are here included as examples as they become rapidly outdated. The idea of office technology being supported by solar has previously played only a very marginal role but now in new glass office buildings the idea has become feasible. Products that are more focused on aesthetics and representation within the workplace could also be seen as applying to private life and many of the products featured in the "Home" and "Light"

chapters could also be incorporated into "Work". Here, it is particularly the characteristics of the product that are determined by what industries or individuals require or wish for. In some cases, the temporary nature of a product is seen as an advantage - the composition is then entirely geared towards the complete recycling of the product - in other cases quality is signaled by the durability of the material.

SafetyNet

Design:
Dan Watson

The SafetyNet was designed to combat overfishing. It exploits fish behavioral habits and physiology to separate different species and ages of fish during the trawling process. The escape rings are reinforcing devices that are fitted into the meshes of the net to hold them wide open. The open holes present an easy and reliable escape route for small fish, which presents a far lower risk of injury to them as they escape. The rings are illuminated like an emergency exit to alert fish to the danger they are in and guide them to the exits. The goal is to use SafetyNet devices in conjunction with legislation to help tackle the issues of bycatch, discarding and unsustainable fishing.

DESIGNERS: Dan Watson (United Kingdom)
YEAR OF DEVELOPMENT: 2012
MAIN MATERIALS: plastic, metal, electronic
MAIN GREEN STRATEGIES: food security,
environmental protection, species
protection

PHOTOS: DAN WATSON. PORTRAIT: TOM BUNNING

Deborah Desk

This classic desk is made from real airplane wings which are transformed by Bedfordshire based company, Reestore Ltd. Entirely handmade in the UK, each Deborah desk is original and crafted from airplane wing panels which are carefully hand riveted into place. The Deborah desk can be customized using different colors or even frosting your company logo or favorite quotes into the glass top to create the perfect personalized desk. This design gives customers a practical desk, which they can adapt with their own bespoke designs and colors. The Deborah desk is only available directly from Reestore.

DESIGNERS: Max Silvana (United Kingdom)
DISTRIBUTOR: Reestore Ltd.
YEAR OF DEVELOPMENT: 2007
MAIN MATERIALS: airplane wing panels, glass
MAIN GREEN STRATEGIES: recycled materials, local production

**Design:
Max Silvana**

Jeremy Table

This unique table is made from an upcycled Rover V8 engine. The Chrome effect coating gives this product a real gleam and touch of glamour - turning it not just into an engine table, but a real eye-catcher as well. Coated with a hardwearing chrome finish it comes with leveling ball and socket height adjustable feet, topped off with an eight-millimeter piece of polished glass. The glass can also be personalized with your name or company logo.

DESIGNERS: Max Silvana (United Kingdom)
DISTRIBUTOR: Reestore Ltd.
YEAR OF DEVELOPMENT: 2012
MAIN MATERIALS: upcycled Rover V8 engine, glass
MAIN GREEN STRATEGIES: recycled materials, local production

Design:
Max Silvana

The Surface Collection

The Surface Collection is a range of smart phone covers made of natural wood or natural leather. They are made in Japan using traditional techniques. The wood cover is one of the world's thinnest wood smartphone covers. Environmentally friendly, it is available in walnut, cedar and teak; using waste wood deemed unsuitable for use as a construction material. The leather cover is made using an 800-year-old traditional leather tanning technique from the Hyogo prefecture in Japan. The cover is cut using the variable cut technique, which preserves the shape and natural beauty of the leather or wood.

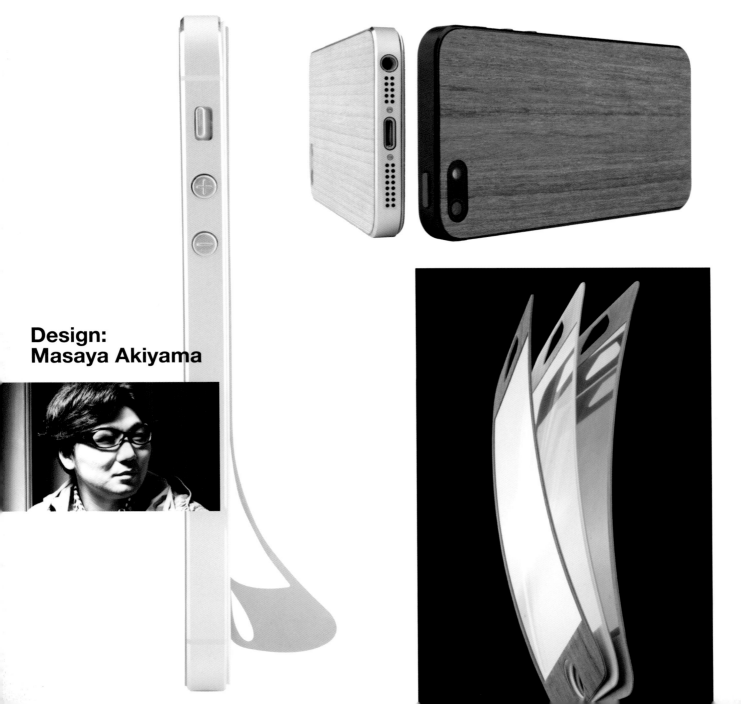

**Design:
Masaya Akiyama**

DESIGNERS: Masaya Akiyama/Colors (Japan)
DISTRIBUTOR: Colors
YEAR OF DEVELOPMENT: 2012
MAIN MATERIALS: natural wood, leather
MAIN GREEN STRATEGIES: natural wood,
thinning wood

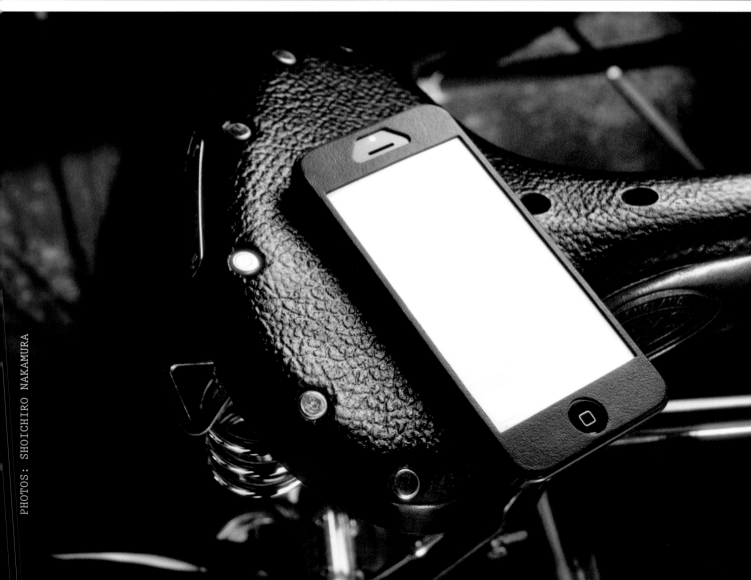

PHOTOS: SHOICHIRO NAKAMURA

Childhood Memories

The Childhood Memories series is made from an unexpected material - crushed eggshells, pressed together to form an object. The first series comprised a stationary set, incorporating a pencil, pencil holder and eraser. All objects in the product range are made of eggshells bound with egg white. The second series includes pencil rings that function as amulets. The products are intended to reflect the fragility of the relationship between humans and nature.

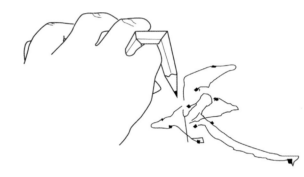

DESIGNERS: Nicolas Cheng (Sweden)
DISTRIBUTOR: Studio Nicolas Cheng
YEAR OF DEVELOPMENT: 2012
MAIN MATERIALS: eggshells, egg white

Design: Nicolas Cheng

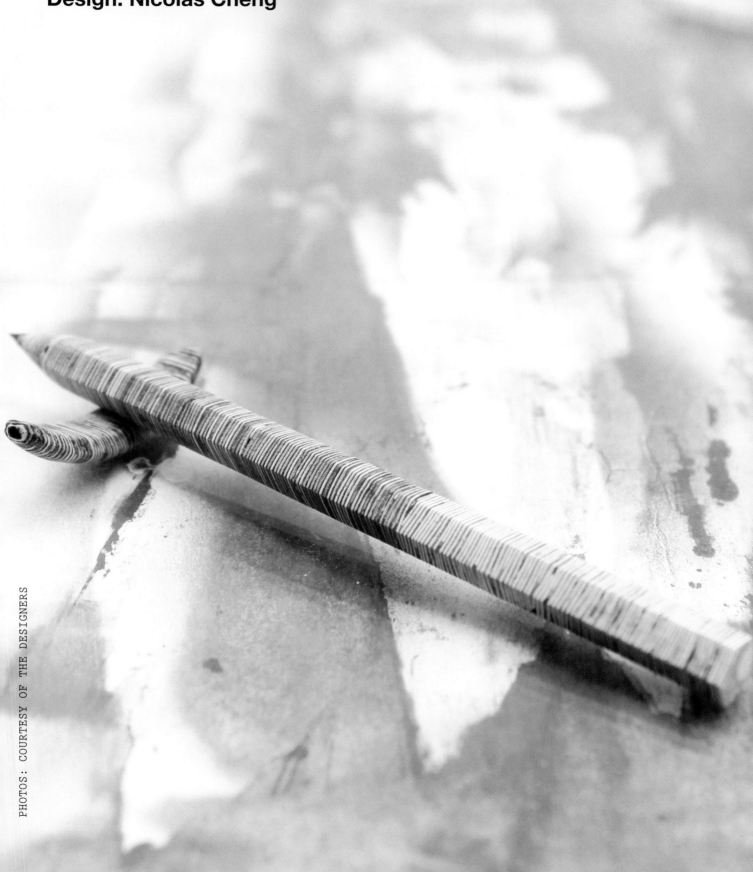

Cutting Table No. 1

This cardboard cutting table was inspired by the designer's experience of constant travel and guerilla studio set-ups that were impeded by one thing - there was no good clean surface on which to work. This light and sturdy corrugated structure was developed to meet the requirements of both the travelling designer and space limited student; or the travelling student and space-limited designer, who need an ergonomic sturdy plane on which to cut, fold, draft, or design. This affordable biodegradable table is easily packed down at the end of the day, enabling the user to regain precious living space.

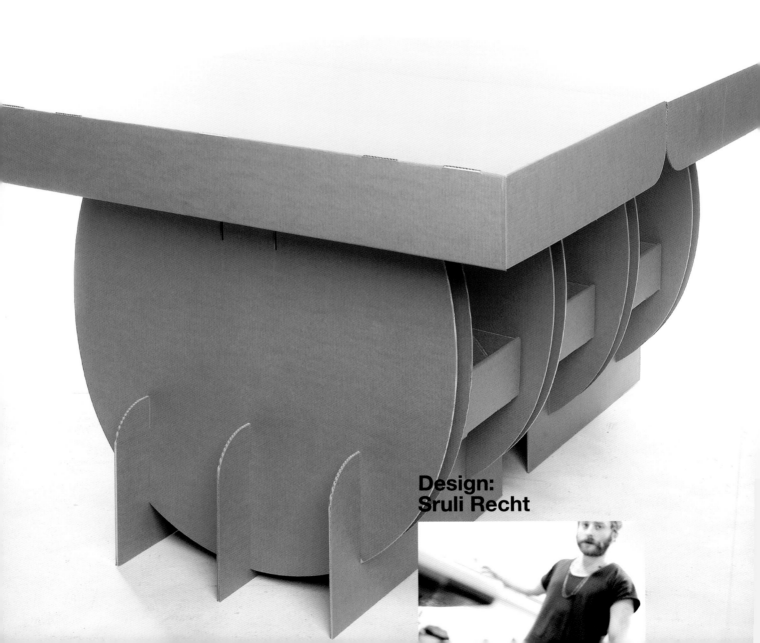

**Design:
Sruli Recht**

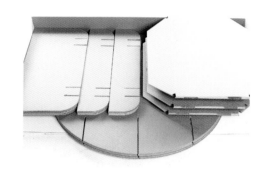

DESIGNERS: Sruli Recht (Iceland)
DISTRIBUTOR: Sruli Recht
YEAR OF DEVELOPMENT: 2008
MAIN MATERIALS: cardboard,
Polyurethane
MAIN GREEN STRATEGIES: recycled
materials, local production, hand
made, durable

Snake Collection

A playful, cheerful and colorful snake with a curvy silhouette, almost like a catoon. Childhood memories led designer Giancarlo Zema to design the new Origami furniture brand; an essential but fun collection that comprises a desk and chair made from recycled dual-colored cardboard. An ideal piece of furniture to decorate smart and eco-friendly homes and offices in a fresh and informal style.

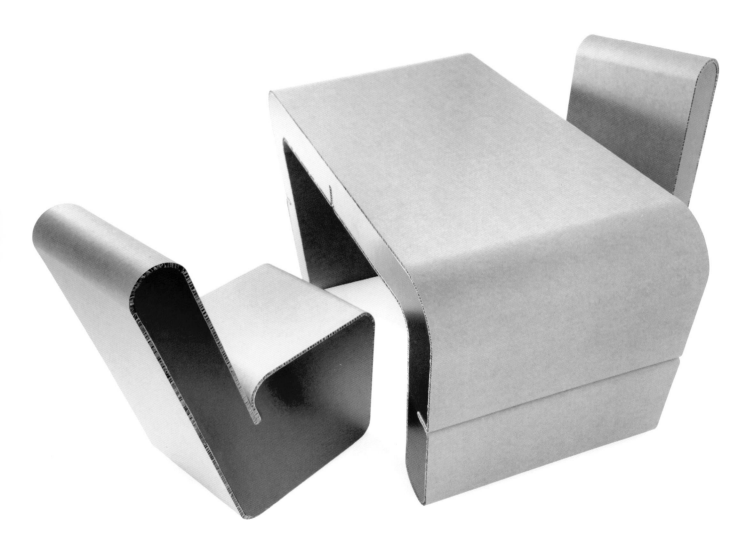

**Design:
Giancarlo Zema**

DESIGNERS:Giancarlo Zema Design Group (Italy)
DISTRIBUTOR: Origami Furniture
YEAR OF DEVELOPMENT: 2013
MAIN MATERIALS: recycled cardboard
MAIN GREEN STRATEGIES: recycling, use of durable
materials

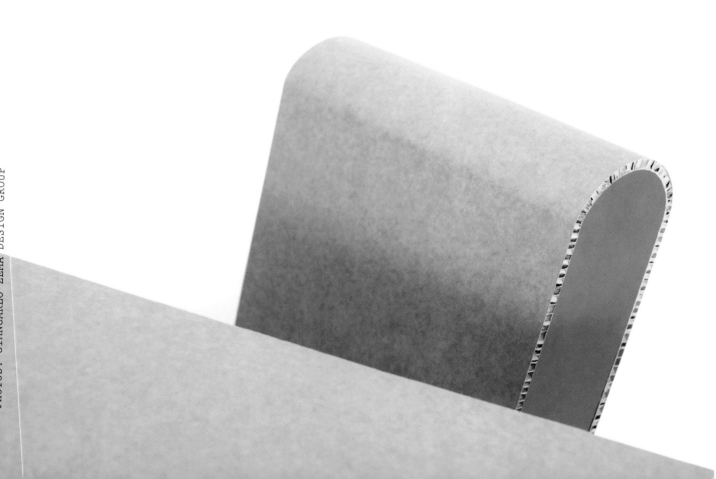

Designers' Index

Imprint

The Deutsche Nationalbibliothek lists
this publication in the Deutsche Natio-
nalbibliografie; detailed bibliographic
data are available in the Internet at
http://dnb.dnb.de

ISBN 978-3-03768-151-0
© 2013 by Braun Publishing AG
www.braun-publishing.ch

1st edition 2013

Coordination:
Editorial office van Uffelen
Layout and text editing: Lisa Rogers,
Natascha Saupe, Sarah Schkölziger,
Chris van Uffelen
Graphic concept: Michaela Prinz